The Music Factory

Teacher Resource Book

Jonathan Rayner

A practical music course for
National Curriculum Key Stage 3/GCSE
General Editor: Jonathan Rayner

FABER ***ff*** MUSIC

© Faber Music Ltd 1993
First published in 1993 by Faber Music Ltd
3 Queen Square London WC1N 3AU
Music and text set by Seton Music Graphics Ltd
Design by James Butler
Cover design by Shirley Tucker
Printed in England by Caligraving Ltd
International copyright secured
All rights reserved

ISBN 0 571 51116 3

Contents

Preface

The Music Factory is a comprehensive, innovative and practical music course, covering Key Stage 3 of the National Curriculum and GCSE. It consists of a **Teacher Resource Book**, a series of interlinked **Instrumental Workbooks** for **Keyboard**, **Guitar**, **Bass Guitar** and **Percussion**, together with a separate volume of **Ensemble Scores**, providing 14 ensemble pieces for use with the Instrumental Workbooks and the Teacher Resource Book.

Teacher Resource Book

The core of **The Music Factory** is a flexible **Teacher Resource Book** containing 120 practical Activities for classroom music-making at Key Stage 3 and GCSE level. The book aims to provide teachers with a comprehensive source of ideas, approaches and starting points for music-making in the classroom. The activities explore a variety of musical styles, and seek to reveal the similarities and individual characteristics of each. Some activities share the same stylistic focus: e.g. there are several which deal with aspects of North Indian classical music, and others which develop the 12-bar blues. The suggested listening at the end of each activity contains, wherever possible, examples from a range of musical cultures.

Structure of the book

The **Teacher Resource Book** is divided into five **chapters**, each based round a particular conceptual area: **Rhythm and Metre**, **Pitch and Melody**, **Harmony**, **Structure and Form**, and **Timbre and Texture**.

Each chapter has four **sections**. In general, the central sections contain material aimed at an average Year 9/10 music class, while the outer ones contain material suitable for Years 7/8 and 11+ respectively. Thus the general progression within each chapter is from elementary to more advances ideas.

Each section contains six main **Activities**, each with variations and extensions on the main idea, together with suggestions for related listening. Each Activity presents a framework for music-making focusing on a particular idea. The Activities involve a range of whole-class, group or individual work. Symbols in the margin denote the nature of the Activity as follows:

 = Whole class activity

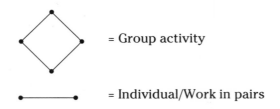

= Group activity

= Individual/Work in pairs

A **P** within the symbol denotes a performance activity; an **L** denotes a listening activity. The absence of a letter denotes types of creative activity, such as experimenting, exploring, improvising, composing, etc., or analysis/appraisal.

How to use the Teacher Resource Book

The book should be used flexibly, as a supporting resource to teachers' own materials and approaches. Although each Activity contains a suggested procedure, teachers might wish to adapt the approaches according to their local needs. Similarly, the order and combination of Activities will vary according to the requirements of individual classes. The author has indicated at the beginning of an Activity if he feels it should be preceded by other preliminary Activities. The Variations and Extensions — which may be used either concurrently, or later for revision and development — are likewise cross-referenced to other Activities.

Instrumental Workbooks

Linked to this Teacher Resource Book is a series of **Instrumental Workbooks** for **Keyboard**, **Guitar**, **Bass Guitar** and **Percussion**. They support and complement the Teacher Resource Book in the following ways:

1. They approach the teaching of musical concepts in similar ways
2. They show how some of the examples quoted in the Resource Book may be played on instruments
3. They contain similar exercises, e.g. question and answer, echo and copycat exercises
4. They develop musicianship skills alongside technique
5. They contain the individual instrumental parts for the Ensemble Pieces
6. They support the performance elements of the National Curriculum and GCSE

Ensemble Scores

A separate volume of **Ensemble Scores**, linked to the Teacher Resource Book and the Instrumental Workbooks, provides 10 original ensemble pieces, 2 arrangements and 2 graphic scores for group performance.

The author would like to thank Rex Billingham, Mark Wyatt, Leonora Davies and Adrian Thorne for their encouragement, advice and support. He is particularly indebted to David Mather for his painstaking and invaluable help in the editorial process and to his editors at Faber Music.

Rhythm and metre

CONTENTS

1

Activities 1–6

1 Pulsations

This activity explores regular beats and the effect of accents within a duple metre.

Procedure

A With students sitting in a circle, give each one a beat number, alternately 1 and 2, around the circle.

B Establish a regular 1–2 beat getting the students to tap the beats silently on the fingertips of their index and middle fingers.

C Get the students to call their beat numbers out aloud against the appropriate finger tap. Each beat group calls their number in unison.

D When this is secure, repeat C with accents on beat 1.

E Make a continuous piece containing sections where, after both beats have been counted aloud, each beat is heard on its own, the other group counting silently. The following structure could be used:

Variations and extensions

i) Repeat the activity using 3 and 4 beats.
ii) Repeat the activity without finger taps.
iii) Repeat the activity with individual students dispersed to the corners of the room.
iv) Repeat *D* but allow students to skip to the adjacent beat. For instance

$$1 - | 1 - | 1 \ 2 | - 2 | - 2 | 1 - | 1 -$$

and so on.

– How did the introduction of silent counts [E] affect the activity?
– What effect did spatial separation [Var.iii] have on the activity?

2 Four square

This activity explores quadruple metre and develops students' skills in rhythmic invention and imitation.

Preparation

This activity calls for a variety of percussion instruments.

Procedure

A Working in a circle, give each student a percussion instrument and a beat number from 1 to 4 in sequence.

B Establish a regular 1–2–3–4 beat and get students to call out their beat numbers, each beat group counting quietly, in unison.

C When this is secure get each student in turn to invent a repeating rhythm (*riff*) on their instrument over the beat count. Use cues to bring in new soloists.

D When the students are familiar with this, get them to count all the beats together in unison in two-bar units — 1234 2234 — and repeat C with each student in turn inventing rhythms to fit within each two-bar unit.

NB. This should be a continuous exercise with a new soloist entering every two bars until all students have had a solo.

Variations and extensions

  i) In *D* use different solo lengths eg. four-bar units.
 ii) Use other metres.
iii) Experiment with faster or slower tempos.
 iv) *Copycat* — In *D* students work in pairs, the first one inventing a simple two-bar rhythm and the second student imitating it. Another student invents a new rhythm and his/her partner copies it, and so on around the circle. Alternatively, the teacher can invent the rhythms with each student copying them in turn around the circle.
  v) *Delayed Copycat* — This is the same as *Copycat* but with a two-bar count between the statement and its copy.

Discussion points

– Was the beat kept regular?
– Which is the easiest tempo for keeping the beats regular — fast, medium or slow?
– Which solos worked best? Why?

3 Backbeat

This activity introduces a basic drum-kit rhythm.

Procedure

A Divide the class into two.

B Start a regular 1–2–3–4 beat.

C Get half the class to tap their right feet on the floor on counts 1 and 3. This is the equivalent of the bass-drum beat.

D Get the remaining half of the class to tap their left hands on their left knees on counts 2 and 4. This is the equivalent of the snare-drum beat, sometimes called the "backbeat".

E Get the two halves to change over.

F Get each student to combine the two rhythms, as shown in the diagram:

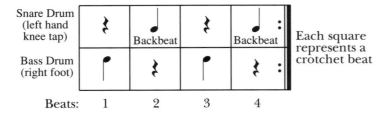

G When this pattern is secure, transfer it on to a drum kit or other instruments.

Variations and extensions

i) *Rhythmic Sandwich*

Get the students to devise repeating rhythms (*riffs*) that go with the one shown above. Combine these into a multi-layered rhythmic texture.

ii) *Rhythmic Programming*

Get the students, individually or in pairs, to programme the pattern shown in the diagram above into a drum machine or sequencer. [Real-time programming is easier at this stage — refer to your machine's manual. Some advice on programming is given in the appendix of each volume of the Percussion Workbooks which complement this book.]

iii) *Changing the Patterns*

The pattern above is very basic and can easily be varied or extended. *Introducing the Hi-Hat*, which forms Activity 11, is itself an extension of this activity and there are further examples in the Percussion Workbooks.

Discussion points

– The main accent is on the first beat of the bar. Why, then, do 2 and 4 seem so strong?

– Try and work out how many of the preset patterns on your drum machine are based on the one above.

– Which other parts of the drum kit are used a lot in preset patterns?

4 Mixed accents

This activity explores the effects of juxtaposing different time signatures.

Procedure

A   Divide the students into two groups.

B   Establish a common regular pulse.

C   Get one group to count in twos, accenting first beats in the normal way: 1, 2, 1, 2 etc. Tapping the beats on fingertips will help, as explained in Activity 1.

D   Bring in the other group counting in threes, again accenting first beats: 1, 2, 3, 1, 2, 3 etc.

E   Repeat *C* and *D* with the groups reversed.

F   Once this is secure, divide the students into four groups and repeat with one group each counting in twos, threes, fours and fives.

Variations and extensions

i)   Get each group to call out their first beats only; the other beats should be counted silently, using the finger tips, for instance.

ii)   Change the groups around.

iii)   Add other metres — sixes, sevens etc.

iv)   *Staggered Starts*

Choose one time signature, $\frac{3}{4}$ for instance, and divide the students into the appropriate number of groups. Get each group to call out the beat in the usual way, with the first beat accented, but start the second group one beat behind the first, and the third one beat behind the second, in the pattern:

Group 1	1 2 3 1 2 3 1 2 3 1 2 3 1 2 3 1 2 3	etc
Group 2	1 2 3 1 2 3 1 2 3 1 2 3 1 2 3 1 2	etc
Group 3	1 2 3 1 2 3 1 2 3 1 2 3 1 2 3 1	etc

v)   Repeat *C/D* and *F*, but with the simple beats of each bar replaced by a more complex one-bar rhythmic pattern invented by the group in question and constantly repeated.

Discussion points

– In *C/D*, how often will all the first beats sound together? [A: every 6 beats] Why?

– Similarly, how often in *F*? [A: every 60 beats].

– Which is harder, *F* or iv)?

– In iv), what difference would it make increasing the number of beats between the start of each group?

5 Più mosso, poco a poco

This activity is designed to develop control over gradual changes in tempo.

Preparation

This activity calls for one or more (see *B*) unpitched percussion instruments.

Procedure

A   Working in a circle, get students to recite the poem *From a railway carriage* by Robert Louis Stevenson. There should be a $\frac{6}{8}$ feel to the recitation, with the predominant rhythmic pattern

$\frac{6}{8}$ ♩♩♩ ♪♩   or $\frac{6}{8}$ ♩♩♩ ♩ ♪ :

Faster than fairies, faster than witches,
Bridges and houses, hedges and ditches,
And charging along like troops in a battle,
All through the meadows, the houses and cattle,
All of the sights of the hill and the plain
Fly as thick as driving rain
And ever again in the wink of an eye,
Painted stations whistle by.

Each line of the poem could be stuck on to flash cards and read by students in turn around the circle.

B   Choose a player (or players) to play an unpitched percussion instrument on the first beat of each $\frac{6}{8}$ bar.
C   Appoint yourself — or one of the students — conductor.
D   Repeat B with the conductor indicating a gradual increase in tempo, as if the train were leaving the station and gathering pace.

Variations and extensions

i) *Meno mosso, poco a poco*
Choose a poem suitable for slowing down rather than speeding up, and repeat D accordingly. An example is the author's *The Tortoise*, which has a $\frac{2}{4}$ beat:

The Tortoise wends its weary way,
Across the hills to work each day,
No sooner there than home to bed,
To soothe its legs and rest its head.

ii) Try repeating D without a conductor.
iii) Transfer the rhythms of the Stevenson poem on to instruments, adding other appropriate sounds, such as the noises made by steam engines.
iv) Get the students to write down the rhythms in some form of notation: they should include symbols or words to show changes in tempo.

Discussion points

– Is it easier to get gradually faster or slower?
– How important is it to have a conductor?
– Did the piece get louder as it got faster? Why?

Further study

Gradual increases and/or decreases in tempo are characteristic of certain Greek and Yugoslav dance music and the end of an Indian raga generally increases gradually in speed [see recommended recording at the end of the next activity].

There are several classical pieces which imitate trains and contain appropriate increases in speed: Honegger's 'Mouvement symphonique No.1', *Pacific 231*; the first and last movements of Prokofiev's suite *Winter Bonfire*; Villa-Lobos' 'Bachiana Brasileira No.2', *The little train of the Caipira*.

6 Indian time cycles (talas)

*This activity introduces some of the time cycles used in Indian Classical music. Indian musicians count beats using claps for the strong beats and their fingers for those in between. A silent wave of the hand (*khali *beat) usually indicates the half-way point of the cycle.*

Procedure

A Get the students to count through the two time cycles shown in the diagrams below. They should clap their hands on the *sam* beats (+), click their fingers on the *tali* beats (∗) and wave the hand (or make some other movement) on the *khali* beats (o); all other beats (•) should be counted silently on the tips of the fingers.

Kerwha Tal

	+	•	•	•	O	•	•	•
Boles	dha	ge	na	tee	ta	ke	dhin	ne

Teen Tal

	+	•	•	•	∗	•	•	•	O	•	•	•	∗	•	•	•
Boles	dha	dhin	dhin	dha	dha	dhin	dhin	dha	dha	thin	thin	tha	tha	dhin	dhin	dha

B Once this is secure, a group of students can recite the *boles*, which Indian drummers (eg. tabla players) use as a guide for their playing.

Variations and extensions

i) Explore various hand sign systems/silent movements to outline the grouping of beats.
ii) Put the *bole* sounds on instruments, the students using these instruments to imitate the sounds of these words as closely as possible.

Discussion points

– Does movement help to establish a beat or cycle of beats?
– Which hand signs/movements work best? Why?

Further study

Activities 14 and 15 of *Pitch and Melody* deal with the basics of Indian *ragas*.

Recordings: *The best of Ravi Shankar and Alla Rakha* (Walkman Classics, DG 415 621–4) [Side 2 track 2 demonstrates the *Teen Tal*]; *Percussion through the ages in South India* (EMI, ECSD 40528)

Book: *Learn to play the tabla*, by R. Avtar'vir' (Pankaj Publications) has more information on *talas*.

Activities 7–12

AIMS

1 To establish and consolidate accurate sub-division and combination of beats, focusing on splits and multiples of two and three.
2 To develop a sense of rhythmic phrasing.
3 To develop individual rhythmic independence and a stronger sense of silent beats.

7 Rhythmic ratatouille

This activity is designed to develop understanding of the division of beats, using the natural rhythm of words.

Preparation

This activity calls for the following list of vegetable names, either on a blackboard or duplicated by some other means:

beans	mushrooms	courgettes	fennel
pumpkin	kale	turnip	parsley
chard	garlic	beetroot	cabbage
leeks	parsnips	swede	radish
groundnuts	marrow	endive	cardoons
sprouts	carrots	peppers	peas
spinach	sweetcorn	cress	lettuce
okra	yams	greens	basil

Further variations for this list are suggested in Var.i) and Var.iv).

Procedure

A Divide the students into groups.
B Get each group to produce a rhythmic ratatouille, made up of a sequence of up to 8 vegetable names taken from the list.
C Get each group in turn to establish a (slow) beat and then to recite its sequence of names, one name starting on each beat.

D   Get each group to clap the rhythms of its words and to identify which have one clap or two.

E   Write the rhythms down using quavers and quaver rests.

Variations and extensions

i)   Replace vegetables with some other class of name: football teams, towns, plants, Christian names, surnames or (for those close enough to London) underground stations. Remember that the names must contain no more than two syllables.

ii) Get each group to change the order of its names, and compare the effect when the new sequence is clapped.

iii) Let each group secretly chose three or four new names from the list, clap the new sequence and see if the others can guess the names.

iv) Try clapping the rhythm of the complete ingredients for ratatouille:

olive oil	garlic
aubergine	onion
courgettes	tomatoes
green pepper	water
freshly ground black pepper	

Discussion points

– Which two-syllable names have a quicker first note [eg. radish], and which an even rhythm [eg. sweetcorn]? Perhaps mention the so-called "Scotch snap" (♪ ♩.).

8 Dividing the beat

This activity is designed to explore quaver divisions of the beat using a poem.

Preparation

This activity calls for a poem whose word rhythm shows a clear quaver beat, such as J.D. Douglas' *RHYTHM*:

> *Pulsating bodies rubbing to the sound of dub RHYTHM.*
> *DJ toasting words are bouncing record scratching RHYTHM.*
> *Finger slapping bassline steady strings vibrating RHYTHM.*
> *Trumpet blearing keyboards twinkling notes are soaring RHYTHM.*
> *Shoulders sliding body poppers dancers breaking RHYTHM.*
> *Belly dancer nipple twister tummy rumbler RHYTHM.*
> *Limbo dancer legs akimbo bamboo crawler RHYTHM.*
> *Runner jumping hurdle strider legs are climbing RHYTHM.*
> *People standing hands are talking body language RHYTHM.*

(from J.D. Douglas' *Caribbean Man's Blues*, Akira Press, 1985)

The poem will need to be copied on a blackboard or on to flash cards and distributed to students.

Some (unpitched) percussion instruments are required for C.

Procedure

A   Get the class to recite the chosen poem in the normal way. It may be easier to have each line recited by a different student.

B   Get the students to work out which words have a natural stress and to mark these accordingly. In the case of our example, the result should be lilting quavers in a $\frac{2}{4}$ metre.

C   Provide some students with percussion instruments and get them to play the quaver rhythm of B, accenting the stressed first beats.

D   Repeat C, now with the remainder of the class reciting the poem.

E   Divide the students into groups and have each work out which parts of the words come on the beat or between beats. They should write down the words using hyphens to show divisions (eg. bo-dies, a-kim-bo).

Variations and extensions

i)   Add movements to the words.

ii) Try writing out the rhythm of the poem using crotchets, quavers and rests.

iii) Think about shaping the piece for performance. Possibilities in the case of our example include: a different voice for each line with a unison refrain of "RHYTHM"; a gradual crescendo; instruments complementing the words; actions.

iv) Try reciting the poem in an *unsuitable* metre (in this case $\frac{3}{4}$) and note the effect on the natural stresses of the lines.

v)   Explore the rhythmic effect of quaver and crotchet rests between phrases, producing patterns such as:

(These, particularly $\frac{5}{8}$, may be found a little too complicated at this stage.)

Discussion points

–   Was there any disagreement about the natural stresses within the poem? If so, why?
–   What tempo is most appropriate for the poem? Why?
–   Discuss the use and effect of an upbeat start.

Further study

For the interaction of rhythm and the spoken words, the following related listening is recommended:

–   Dub poets, such as Jean Binta Breeze, Benjamin Zephaniah
–   Rapping/toasting
–   Walton's *Façade* [the original *Entertainment*, not the subsequent orchestral suites]

9 Rhythmic counterpoint

This activity is designed to develop rhythmic independence by holding one pattern against several others.

Preparation

Instruments as appropriate, and copies of the rhythm bank (A).

Procedure

A   Get the students to clap/play in unison each of the following four-bar rhythmic phrases in $\frac{3}{4}$:

	1 2 3	2 2 3	3 2 3	4 2 3
1	♩ ♩ ♩	♩ ♩ ♩	♩ ♩ ♩	♩ ♩ ♩
2	♩.	♩.	♩.	♩ ♩ ♩
3	♩ ♩	♩ ♩	♩ ♩	♩ ♩ ♩
4	♩ ♩	♩ ♩	♩ ♩	♩ ♩ ♩
5	♩ ♩ ♫	♩ ♩ ♫	♩ ♩ ♫	♩ ♩ ♩
6	♩ ♫ ♩	♩ ♫ ♩	♩ ♫ ♩	♩ ♩ ♩
7	♫ ♩ ♩	♫ ♩ ♩	♫ ♩ ♩	♩ ♩ ♩
8	♩ ♫ ♫	♩ ♫ ♫	♩ ♫ ♫	♩ ♩ ♩
9	♫ ♫ ♩	♫ ♫ ♩	♫ ♫ ♩	♩ ♩ ♩
10	♫ ♫ ♫	♫ ♫ ♫	♫ ♫ ♫	♩ ♩ ♩

B   Divide the students into four groups and play/clap through a sequence of rhythmic phrases in the form of a round, groups entering at one-bar intervals.

C   Divide the students into a maximum of 10 smaller groups and assign to each a different phrase taken from the above. A conductor (either the teacher or a selected student) then signals groups to enter with their rhythm or to stop, being careful to do this only at the divisions between four-bar phrases.

Variations and extensions

i)   Add a four-bar chord progression, such as Cmaj[7], Am[7], Fmaj[7], G[11]

ii) Try giving pitches to some of the rhythmic phrases, using, for instance, the partial scale CDEFG or pentatonic scale CDEGA, which fit with chords in i) above.

iii) Add stresses to some of the notes.
iv) Repeat *C*, but with new rhythmic phrases in a different metre.
v) As iv) but incorporate rests in the rhythmic phrases.

Discussion points

– How difficult is it to hold one rhythm against another?
– Was the piece rhythmically tight? How could ensemble be improved?
– Which instruments suit which lines of the piece?

10 Question and answer

This activity is designed to develop skill at imitation and response.

Procedure

A Gather the students into a circle and choose one to act as timekeeper. (A metronome or equivalent could be used instead.)

B Against the timekeeper's steady beat, clap/play a one- or two-bar rhythm using minims, crotchets and quavers, which the students as a class immediately copy. For instance:

C Repeat *B* with different rhythms, until secure. Selected students may take over as leader.
D Clap/play rhythms as above, getting individual students to provide answering rhythms, as:

Leader: Question   Student: Answer

Question and Answer should always be of the same length. Try to avoid gaps between Question and Answer and to make Answers as spontaneous as possible.
E Go round the circle with students inventing Question and Answer phrases alternately.

Variations and extensions

i) Change the metre.
ii) Change the tempo.
iii) Use longer phrases.
iv) Go round the circle in fours, as follows:
      1 invents a rhythmic phrase
      2 provides an Answer
      3 copies 1
      4 copies 2

– Which were the most pleasing answering ideas? Why?

11 Introducing the hi-hat

This activity is a follow-up to Activity 3, Backbeat.

Procedure

A   Revise the basic activity (steps A–F) of *Backbeat* (Activity 3).

B   When the right-foot and left-hand rhythms are secure, introduce a new pattern —
the right hand tapping the right knee in quavers. This simulates the hi-hat rhythm,
as follows:

right knee	Hi-hat	♫	♫	♫	♫
left knee	snare drum	𝄽	♩	𝄽	♩
right foot	bass drum	♩	𝄽	♩	𝄽

NB. Before each student can cope with all of this simultaneously, it may be necessary
to try the pattern out with each rhythm played by a different group. The groups can
be rotated until the whole pattern has been experienced in parts.

C   Once all three rhythms are secure, transfer them to the drum kit or other instruments.

D   Introduce the "fill-in" bar, which will act as the last bar of a four- or eight-bar phrase.
Over bass-drum crotchets, quaver pairs should be tapped out as follows:

high tom	𝄽	♫	𝄽	𝄽
mid tom	𝄽	𝄽	♫	𝄽
low tom	𝄽	𝄽	𝄽	♫
snare drum	♫	𝄽	𝄽	𝄽
bass drum	♩	♩	♩	♩

NB. When incorporating these patterns into *B* above, tap the snare and tom tom
patterns on the knee, or vocalise the drum sounds.

E   When the "fill-in" bar is secure, construct a repeating four-bar phrase out of three
repetitions of the *B* pattern followed by the "fill-in" bar.

Variations and extensions

i) Add a chord sequence such as I–VI–IV–V. (Activity 10 of *Harmony* deals with this common progression.)

ii) Change the tempo.

iii) *Rhythmic Programming*

Get the students, individually or in pairs, to programme the pattern shown in the diagrams above into a drum machine or sequencer. [Some advice on programming is given in the appendix to each volume of the Percussion Workbooks which complement this book.]

iv) Try varying the bass drum pattern in B to $\left|\begin{smallmatrix}4\\4\end{smallmatrix}\right.$ ♩ ⁷♪♩ ♩ ‖

or $\left|\begin{smallmatrix}4\\4\end{smallmatrix}\right.$ ♩ ♩ ♫♩ ♩ ‖

12 Timeless

This activity is designed to explore sounds without a sense of beat.

Preparation

This activity calls for pitched instruments capable of sustaining notes.

Procedure

A   Divide the students into three or four groups.

B   Let each group choose a set of pitched instruments and a single note (or two nearby notes) to play.

C   Get each group to sustain its note(s) indefinitely, the players overlapping so that no gaps are heard.

Variations and extensions

i) Repeat *C* with the groups entering in a predetermined order and following a predetermined dynamic contour.

ii) Where considerable space is available, experiment with spatial effects.

iii) A student (or students in turn) should take the role of conductor, bringing groups in and out at will.

iv) Repeat *C*, using it as a background for occasional rhythmic ideas and/or random accents. Take care these are not so frequent or intrusive that they destroy the "timeless" quality of the piece.

Discussion points

– Which instruments can sustain notes most easily?

– How do instruments which cannot sustain easily give an impression of long sounds? (The instrumental workbooks which complement this book contain examples.)

– Which combination of instruments works best? Why?

Further study

"Timeless" music is to be found:
- at the beginning of *Shine on you Crazy Diamond*, from Pink Floyd's album *Wish you were here*
- throughout Stockhausen's *Stimmung*
- in the beginning section (the *alap*) of an Indian *raga*

How does each piece create its feeling of timelessness?

Activities 13—18

AIMS
1 To develop and consolidate accurate placing of off-beat notes.
2 To introduce triplet, dotted and syncopated rhythms.
3 To develop and consolidate rhythmic independence within polyrhythmic textures

13 The triplet

This activity is designed to introduce the triplet rhythm —

Preparation

This activity calls for the sheet music and/or a commercial recording of a well-known song whose tune features a triplet rhythm prominently in the first phrase. Useful examples are Lionel Bart's *Food, glorious Food*:

or Rogers and Hammerstein's Getting to know you:

Possibly less familiar examples are included as recommended listening under *Further study*.

Procedure

A   Get the class to sing the selected song.

B   Let one or two students tap out a steady beat, then get the remainder to clap out the rhythm of the first phrase of the song. It may be helpful to tell the students to imagine the tune being sung in their heads as they clap.

C   Isolate the triplet figure, and get the class to tap the crotchet beat on their left knees and the triplet rhythm on their right knees. Again it may be a help to think of words from the selected tune which take a triplet rhythm: for instance, "glo-ri-ous" or "get-ting to".

Variations and extensions

i)   Repeat the knee-tapping of C, but with the whole first phrase of the selected tune, not just the isolated triplet.

ii) *Triplet Echo*
Divide the students into five groups. Get one group to establish a steady $\frac{4}{4}$ beat; then bring in the remaining groups in the following repeating four-bar pattern:

iii) *Triplet Echo* can be varied by:
– dispersing the groups around the room for spatial effect.
– extending the pattern, so that the echo is delayed further.
– expanding the pattern to make eight-bar phrases.

iv) Repeat *Introducing the Hi-Hat* (Activity 11), using triplets instead of quavers in the "fill-in" bar (D).

Further study

Other items with prominent and accessible triplet rhythms include:
– Tchaikovsky's Sixth Symphony (second movement, main theme)
– Holst's suite *The Planets* (opening of Mars)
– Ravel's *Bolero* (side drum rhythm)
– Vangelis' theme tune to *Chariots of Fire*
– *Maria* from Bernstein's *West Side Story*
– Murray and Callender's *Ballad of Bonnie and Clyde*

14 Dotted rhythms

This activity is designed to introduce dotted rhythms.

Procedure

A   Gather the students into a circle.
B   Establish a slow crotchet beat ($\downarrow$ = 60), then pass this round the circle, each student in turn clapping one crotchet.

C When this is secure and regular, pass quavers round the circle, each student clapping a pair.

D Repeat with groups of four semiquavers.

E Repeat *D*, stressing the first and last semiquavers of each group.

F Repeat *E*, leaving out the unstressed notes and lengthening the first note to produce the dotted rhythm 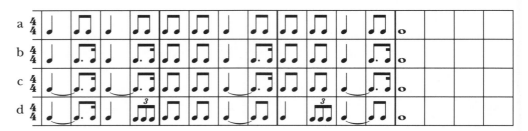 .

Variations and extensions

i) Try setting faster and slower beats.

ii) Get the students to tap/clap through the following rhythmic patterns in order:

iii) After ii), play a recording (or just the tune) of Fauré's *Pavane*, Op.50, which uses all these rhythms.

Pavane (Theme)

Gabriel Fauré

iv) Play through an Irish hornpipe, for instance *The Greencastle*, which is included in Activity 11 of *Structure and Form*.

Further study

The following related listening all contains prominent dotted rhythms:
- The scherzo of Beethoven's *Hammerklavier* Sonata
- *Montagues and Capulets* from the Second Suite Prokofiev made from his ballet *Romeo and Juliet*
- Purcell's *Trumpet Air*
- some Boogie-Woogie piano music uses dotted-rhythm bass figures, for instance Meade Lux Lewis' *Honky Tonk Train Blues* and pieces by Pete Johnson

15 Reggae feel

This activity explores the use of chords placed on off-beats, which is one of the principal features of most reggae music.

Preparation

This activity calls for:
- a recording of Bob Marley's *One Love* (from the album *Legend*, Island BMW 1)
- pitched instruments

Some preliminary work on triads is necessary — see *Harmony*, in particular Activity 8, which introduces chords I, IV and V.

Procedure

A   Play Bob Marley's *One Love*, getting the students to concentrate on the chords in the chorus section and to notice how these are placed *between* the main beats, on quaver off-beats.

B   Appoint a timekeeper (or timekeepers) and divide the remainder of the class into three groups with pitched instruments.

C   Give each group the notes of one of the three primary triads I, IV and V.

D   Get the timekeeper(s) to set a steady $\frac{4}{4}$ pulse at about ♩ = 72.

E   Get each group in turn to play its chord on the quaver off-beats (one — **and** — two — **and** etc.) for two bars in the order I, IV, V:

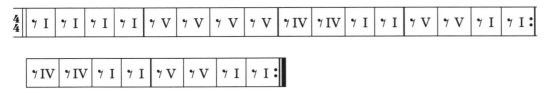

F   When this is secure, play through the chord progression for the chorus of *One Love*:

$\frac{4}{4}$ | ⅄ I | ⅄ I | ⅄ I | ⅄ I | ⅄ V | ⅄ V | ⅄ V | ⅄ V | ⅄ IV | ⅄ IV | ⅄ I | ⅄ I | ⅄ V | ⅄ V | ⅄ I | ⅄ I :||

| ⅄ IV | ⅄ IV | ⅄ I | ⅄ I | ⅄ V | ⅄ V | ⅄ I | ⅄ I :||

G   Pick a small vocal group and repeat *F* with the melody sung against the chords.

Variations and extensions

i) Try working out the chord pattern for the verse of *One Love*.
ii) Using a neighbour-note chord progression such as A minor — G major, invent simple bass riffs around the triad notes along the lines of:

Chords: 𝄾 Am 𝄾 Am 𝄾 Am 𝄾 Am 𝄾 G 𝄾 G 𝄾 G 𝄾 G
Beats: **1 + 2 + 3 + 4 + 1 + 2 + 3 + 4 +**

Neighbour-note chord progressions are dealt with in Activity 12 of *Harmony*.
iii) Make a reggae version of a well-known song, such as Bacharach's *Walk on by*.

16 The calypso beat

This activity introduces a rhythm which is fundamental to calypso, Latin American and much popular music.

Procedure

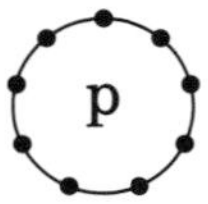

A With the students working in a circle, establish a steady pulse.
B Get the students in turn to call out the beats of a $\frac{4}{4}$ bar, plus an off-beat "and", thus:

student	*call*	*student*	*call*
1	one and	6	two and
2	two and	7	three and
3	three and	8	four and
4	four and	9	one and
5	one and		*and so on . . .*

(With large classes, it may be more practical to have the beats called by small groups placed in a circle rather than by individuals.)
C Repeat *B* until each student has experienced every number. With an odd number of students, simply go round the circle four times without a break. With an even number of students it will be necessary to make four separate circuits, starting each time with the next student along. (Where groups are being used, there should be an odd number.)
D Repeat, replacing the calling of numbers with the following clapped rhythm, each student in turn taking a crotchet segment around the circle:

E Repeat *D*, omitting the first quaver of the second beat:

F   Get the whole class to call out the beats and clap this last rhythm in unison.

G   Increase the tempo.

H   Repeat with foot taps replacing the calling-out of beats.

I   Get the class to sing through a well-known calypso song, such as *Jamaica Farewell*, whilst tapping or clapping the rhythm of E.

Variations and extensions

The rhythm introduced here is further developed in the next activity.

Further study

Listen to the bass line of Ben E. King's *Stand by Me* which uses the related rhythm:

17 Latin and African counterpoints

This activity extends the rhythm introduced in Activity 16 into a new pattern, and explores its use as a time-keeper in the highly rhythmic music of Africa and Latin America.

Preparation

This activity calls for the percussion instruments listed under *C* and *D*, or reasonable substitutes, while the ancillary sections require pitched instruments.

Procedure

A   Revise Activity 16.

B   Using similar procedures, introduce an extension to that rhythm as follows:

C Distribute the necessary instruments and assemble the following rhythmic pattern, which is characteristic of the Cuban dance called the Mambo:

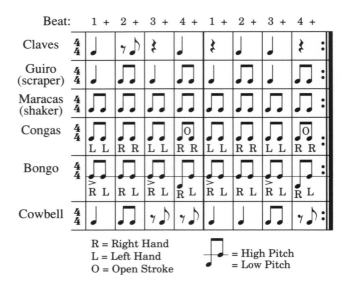

R = Right Hand
L = Left Hand
O = Open Stroke

= High Pitch
= Low Pitch

Note how the claves use the rhythm from *B*.

D Distribute the necessary instruments and assemble the following rhythmic pattern, which is characteristic of the Kpanlogo style from West Africa:

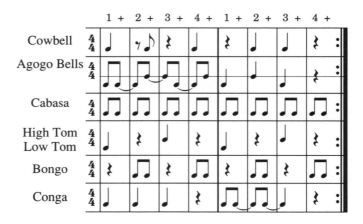

Variations and extensions

 i) Transfer these rhythms on to pitched instruments.
ii) Structure the pieces to include solo sections.

Further study

The following related listening is recommended:

Latin American
– Dance Mania by Tito Puente and his Orchestra (Carino DBL 1–5017)
– Hits by Tito Rodrigues (WS-Latino WSLA 4060)

African
- side 2 track 4 of *Womad Talking Book — an introduction*
- *Mustapha Tettey Addy* (Tangent, TGS 113)

The Latin-American style is also parodied in the introduction to *America* from Leonard Bernstein's *West Side Story* and in Noel Coward's song [*Señorita*] *Nina*.

18 Syncopations

This activity is designed to introduce syncopation through examination of ragtime rhythms.

Preparation

This activity calls for a commercial recording and/or sheet music of Scott Joplin's *Maple Leaf Rag*.

Procedure

A Appoint two time keepers and establish them in a steady, slowish ($\quad$ = about 60) $\frac{2}{4}$ pulse.

B Get the remainder of the class to clap through the following rhythms:

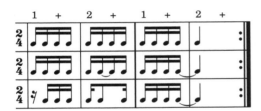
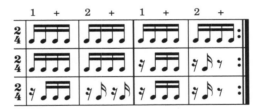

C Play them the first section of Scott Joplin's *Maple Leaf Rag*.
D Get the students to identify which of the above rhythms are used in the melody.

Variations and extensions

i) Get the students to invent questions and answers after the manner of Activity 10, using syncopated rhythms.

Further study

Activity 18 of *Structure and Form* deals with the form of *Maple Leaf Rag*.

There is plenty of printed and recorded music in rag style, which also spread its influence as far as Debussy (*Golliwogg's Cake Walk* from the suite *Children's Corner*) and Stravinsky (*Ragtime* from the music for *The Soldier's Tale*).

Activities 19—24

> **AIMS**
> 1 To introduce and explore compound and irregular metres.
> 2 To explore the effect of accents on weak beats.
> 3 To develop rhythmic independence still further.

19 Swing

This activity introduces swung rhythms, which are a cross between dotted and triplet rhythms.

Preparation

This activity calls for the sheet music and commercial recording(s) of a well-known song which is widely used in jazz music. The song in question should be one notated in dotted rhythms customarily "swung". The following is all based on the example of *Fascinatin' Rhythm* by George and Ira Gershwin. There are recordings of *Fascinatin' Rhythm* by Ella Fitzgerald with Nelson Riddle, by Fred and Adele Astaire (recorded in London back in April 1926 with Gershwin himself at the piano), and Yehudi Menuhin with Stéphane Grappelli.

Procedure

A Select a well-known tune which is widely used in jazz.
B Give the students a representative portion of the tune's rhythm, as it is written down in the score:

C Establish an appropriate (minim) beat and get the class to clap this rhythmic phrase.
D Play a recording of this song, asking the students to compare the way in which the phrase above is written down with how it is sung.
E Clap through the rhythm above using dotted and triplet patterns, as follows:

F Get the class to compare these two new variants with the recording. (Swung rhythms are slightly closer to triplets than to dotted figures.)

Variations and extensions

i) Give the students the "straight" printed rhythms of other well-known jazz standards (such as the Ellington/Strayhorn *Satin Doll*), and get them to swing the rhythms.

ii) If appropriate to the choice of tune at *A*, discuss features of its structure: in the case of *Fascinatin' Rhythm*, the repeated figure of six quavers, each recurrence arriving a quaver earlier than expected.

Further study

There is plenty of "Swing" music in the jazz of the 1930s, in particular in the Big-Band music of Benny Goodman, Count Basie and Artie Shaw, and in the smaller combos led by Fats Waller or Teddy Wilson.

20 Compound metres

This activity is designed to introduce compound time by examining a $\frac{6}{8}$ Irish jig.

Preparation

This activity requires parts for the following arrangement of *The Irish Washerwoman*:

The Irish Washerwoman

♩ = c.120

Trad. arr. Rayner

Rhythm and Metre

Procedure

A   Refer back to *The Triplet* (Activity 13), and revise up to step D.

B   Get the class to repeat this, emphasising every other tap on the left knee. This produces a $\frac{6}{8}$ rhythm, with two dotted crotchet beats on the left knee and 2×3 quavers on the right.

C   When this is secure, get the class to play through *The Irish Washerwoman*.

Variations and extensions

i)   Clap through some of the commoner rhythmic patterns associated with $\frac{6}{8}$. Then try to identify these in well-known tunes, for instance *Greensleeves*, *One more river* and *Ye banks and braes* (the last two, with other examples, can be found in Brocklehurst's *Pentatonic Songbook*).

ii)   Make up vocalisations for the rhythms, for instance "Do-ba-be" or "De-ba-be", which underline the main accents. Use them to help learn some of the common $\frac{6}{8}$ rhythmic figures.

iii)   Invent a 12-bar blues with $\frac{12}{8}$ shuffle rhythm. (The 12-bar blues is discussed in Activity 9 of *Structure and Form*; for details on shuffle drum patterns, see the Percussion Instrumental Workbook which complements this book.)

iv)   Compare the structure of *The Irish Washerwoman*, above, with that of *The Greencastle*, the hornpipe which may have been used in connection with Activity 14. (This topic is covered in Activity 11 of *Structure and Form*.)

Discussion points

– What effect does the upbeat have?

– Discuss the difference between $\frac{6}{8}$ and $\frac{3}{4}$ metres.

Further study

Ensemble Piece No.6 is in the style of a $\frac{12}{8}$ blues shuffle. The score can be found in the separate *Ensemble Scores* volume and the parts in Unit 13 of the instrumental workbooks which complement this volume.

Music in compound time is very common. Irish jigs may be found on records by The Chieftains, while $\frac{6}{8}$ figures prominently in gigues from Baroque suites (for instance, Bach's Third Orchestral Suite) or in Mozart "hunting" finales (such as those of the Third and Fourth Horn Concertos). *Memory* from the musical *Cats* by Andrew Lloyd-Webber is a good example of the use of 12/8.

21 Three against two

This activity explores how the grouping of notes within a bar affects the metre. It concentrates on the difference between $\frac{6}{8}$ and $\frac{3}{4}$.

Procedure

A Remind the students of the calypso rhythm introduced in Activity 16. One way of understanding this rhythm is to think of it as three unequal groups of quavers:

<u>1</u> 2 3 <u>4</u> 5 6 <u>7</u> 8   or   <u>1</u> 2 3 <u>1</u> 2 3 <u>1</u> 2

You could think of this rhythm as two bars of $\frac{3}{8}$ and one of $\frac{2}{8}$.

B Get the students to count eight beats and clap on the numbers underlined above.

C Get the students to clap the two beats of a $\frac{6}{8}$ bar, on quavers 1 and 4.

D Introduce a second bar where the quavers are grouped in twos, creating a $\frac{3}{4}$ bar:

<u>1</u> 2 3 <u>4</u> 5 6 <u>1</u> 2 <u>3</u> 4 <u>5</u> 6

E Once this is secure, divide the class into small groups. Get each group in turn to play the following pattern, half the students clapping the upper, the remainder the lower part. Make sure all the groups count in with a six-beat introduction.

Count in bar: 1 2 3 4 5 6

F Get the groups to clap through rhythms such as the following, in sequence and/or contrapuntally:

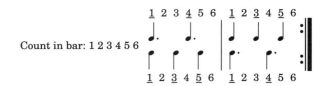

Variations and extensions

i) Play a recording of *America* from Bernstein's *West Side Story*. Get the students to identify the rhythms being used. Then sing it through.

Further study

Ensemble Piece No.9 includes crotchet triplets in $\frac{4}{4}$ time. The score can be found in the separate *Ensemble Scores* volume and the parts in Unit 19 of the instrumental work-books which complement this volume.

22 Irregular stresses

This activity explores the effect of placing stresses on weak beats of a bar.

Procedure

A Divide the students into two groups.

B Get one group to count four beats aloud, clapping on the first beat of each bar (as underlined).

C Get the second group to count the beats silently, clapping only those marked with an accent:

       > >   >   >   >   >

<u>1</u> 2 3 4 <u>1</u> 2 3 4 <u>1</u> 2 3 4 <u>1</u> 2 3 4 <u>1</u> 2 3 4 <u>1</u> 2 3 4 <u>1</u> 2 3 4 <u>1</u> 2 3 4

D Get the groups to swap over.

E Repeat with pairs or smaller groups.

Variations and extensions

i) Play a recording of *Auguries of Spring* from the first part of Stravinsky's *Rite of Spring* (LAM 91), from where this pattern of accents is taken. Discuss the effect of irregular stresses.

ii) Add chords to the rhythms. The first group takes a chord of B^7 with its root the B an octave below middle C; the second group uses a chord of C, starting two octaves below middle C.

23 Irregular metres

This activity explores irregular rhythms, in particular $\frac{7}{8}$.

Preparation

This activity calls for a commercial recording of Dave Brubeck's *Unsquare Dance* (on the album *Greatest Hits*, CBS 40–32046, or CDCBS 32046). In addition it would be useful for the rhythmic patterns in *D* to be written on a blackboard or duplicated by some other means, ready for *E* and *F*.

Procedure

A Gather the students into a circle.

B Establish a regular beat grouped in sevens and get the students to call out the beat numbers in turn around the circle. Unless the total number of students is a multiple of 7, seven times round the circle will ensure each student has called every number.

C When this is secure, repeat with silent beats in agreed places, for instance:

1 – – 4 – – – or 1 – – – 5 – –.

D Get the students to clap through the following patterns:

$$\frac{7}{8}\ \flat\gamma\flat\gamma\gamma\flat\gamma\gamma\, \sqcap :\|\qquad \frac{7}{8}\ \downarrow\ \downarrow\ \downarrow.\ :\|\qquad \frac{7}{8}\ \downarrow\ \downarrow\ \downarrow\ \flat :\|$$

$$\frac{7}{8}\ \gamma\flat\gamma\flat\gamma\ \sqcap :\|\qquad \frac{7}{8}\ \downarrow.\ \downarrow\ \downarrow\ :\|\qquad \frac{7}{8}\ \sqcap\flat\sqcap\sqcap :\|$$

E Listen to Dave Brubeck's *Unsquare Dance*.

F Get the students to identify the rhythmic pattern used for the bass part and then of the hand claps.

Variations and extensions

i) The rhythms identified in *F* could be clapped contrapuntally by two groups; once this is secure, the whole pattern could be tapped on the right and left knees as follows:

ii) See if the students can work out the rhythms used in the piano tune of *Unsquare Dance*; also the pitches used in the bass line.

iii) Experiment with variations of the bass rhythm:

1 2 3 <u>4</u> 5 <u>6</u> 7   or   1 2 <u>3</u> 4 5 <u>6</u> 7

Further study

The following related listening is recommended:

$\frac{5}{8}$ and $\frac{5}{4}$

- Brubeck's *Take Five* (also on the *Greatest Hits* album)
- The ostinato figure from *Mars* in Holst's suite *The Planets*.

$\frac{7}{8}$

- The Stranglers' *Golden Brown*, which alternates between $\frac{7}{8}$ and $\frac{6}{8}$.
- The Greek national dance *Kalamatianos* is in $\frac{7}{8}$.
- The last movement of Prokofiev's Seventh Piano Sonata is in $\frac{7}{8}$ (2 + 3 + 2) throughout.
- The last movement of Shostakovich's Second Piano Concerto has an uninhibited second subject in $\frac{7}{8}$ (Fig.41ff.)

24 Moving accents

This activity explores rhythmic patterns which move out of phase with each other.

Procedure

A Get the students to invent a simple one-bar rhythm, using quavers and quaver rests, such as:

B Divide the class into two groups. Both groups begin playing the chosen rhythm together, but gradually move out of synchronisation: after every eight bars the second group omits a single quaver, getting by so much ahead of the first group. This is best managed by writing the new rhythms out after the manner of the following:

The first group plays the line marked a) throughout. The second group plays each line in succession eight times. The piece ends when the second groups arrives at i), which is the same as a), so the two groups *should* be playing identical patterns. It is necessary to decide in advance how many times the original rhythm will be played in unison to end the piece, and it may be helpful to make use of a conductor. (In the diagram above, b) is formed by taking the first quaver from a) and moving it to the end. The same process is repeated throughout: thus the quaver rest at the beginning of c) becomes the quaver rest at the end of d).)

C   Repeat, dividing the students into smaller groups.

Variations and extensions

i) Repeat with a different rhythm.
ii) Tape the part played by the first group in *B*, ie. 72 repetitions of the rhythm in *A*. Students, working individually or in pairs, could then work through the piece against the tape.

Further study

Several works by Steve Reich which use the "phase" technique, have been recorded. They include *Clapping Music* (Nonesuch 979 169–1) and *Violin Phase* (ECM 1168).

Pitch and melody

CONTENTS

33

Activities 1–6

 AIMS

1. To establish and consolidate a perception of pitch relationships within a narrow pitch range.
2. To introduce some limited pitch scales: the partial major scale (*d r m f s*) and the major pentatonic (*d r m s l*).
3. To develop imitative and call-and-response skills.
4. To develop pitch memory skills.
5. To introduce graphic and short-stave notations.

1 S–A–T–B

This activity is designed to explore relative pitch ranges and to establish an awareness of the ranges of various voice types.

Procedure

A Working in a circle, get each student in turn to sing the highest pitch they can manage *comfortably*.

B Of these highest notes decide whose is the highest and whose the lowest in pitch.

C Repeat A and B with each student's lowest comfortable note.

D Divide the students into pairs (or suitably small groups).

E Get each pair/group to plot, using a pitched instrument of some kind, the highest and lowest pitches of each individual student, marking the result on a pitch graph such as:

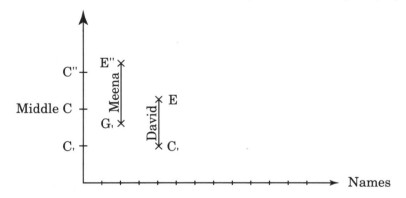

F Reunite the class and collate the results on a master pitch graph.

G Discuss the implications of the results.

H Introduce and explain the terms soprano, contralto, tenor and bass. It is important to stress that most people's voices lie naturally in the areas where these overlap, ie. in the mezzo-soprano or baritone ranges. With older classes some explanation of the phenomenon of falsetto might be appropriate.

Variations and extensions

i) Illustrate *H* with recordings of each or some of these voice types. It would make comparison clearer if the extracts were all in the same key.

ii) Extend i) by asking the class to pick the highest and lowest notes sung by each singer: they are most readily remembered by the word or phrase sung at the time. These notes can be identified and plotted as in *E* above.

iii) Introduce and discuss the more unusual or extreme voice types: coloratura soprano, counter-tenor, basso profundo. There are many examples of all of these in music from the 17th and 18th centuries, for instance (respectively) the Queen of the Night from Mozart's *The Magic Flute*, virtually any Handel operatic "hero", and Seneca from Monteverdi's *The Coronation of Poppea*.

iv) Repeat *E* and *F* with instruments rather than voices.

Discussion points

– Were some voiced pitches difficult to find on a pitched instrument? Why should this be?

Further study

There is an abundance of recorded music by voices of these various types, but arias by Bach and Handel provide simple, direct and, above all, accessible examples. Popular singers fitting the main voice types include:

> *soprano*: Julie Andrews, Barbra Streisand, Whitney Houston, Kate Bush
> *contralto*: Nina Simone, Joan Armatrading
> *tenor*: Stevie Wonder, Billy Joel
> *bass*: Barry White, Topol, Paul Robeson

Of vocalists with a particularly extended range Bobby McFerrin and the legendary Yma Sumac stand out.

2 Approximate pitching

This activity looks at styles of music which use approximate pitching rather than exact pitches.

Preparation

This activity calls for copies of the lyrics of a rap. It would be helpful also to have a commercial recording of the rap and a tape recorder. The ancillary sections require commercial recordings of Walton's *Façade* [NB. the original "entertainment" for reciter and small ensemble, not the subsequent orchestral suites](var.i) and of Schoenberg's *Pierrot Lunaire*.

Procedure

A   Get a student to perform the rap, or alternatively play a commercial recording. As the piece has to be given identically several times during what follows, it might be helpful, where a student's performance is to be used, to record this either at this point or in advance.

B Ask the students to listen for the points where the performer uses the highest and the lowest pitches and to mark on their copies of the lyrics the words or parts of words where this happens. Repeat *A*.

C Again making use of the recording, get the students to make a graphic score of the pitches used in each line of the rap. Many of them will be approximately the same.

D Divide the students into small groups.

E Get each group to choose its own rap and produce a graphic score.

F Exchange the graphs produced at *E* between the groups.

G Get each group in turn to perform the rap given to it according to the graph produced by the group concerned.

Variations and extensions

i) Play a recording of some pieces from Walton's *Façade*. Compare the technique to that of the rap. The reciter's part in *Façade* has only its rhythm notated, no pitches.

ii) Try performing a piece from *Façade*.

iii) Compare the techniques used in rap and in *Façade* with the *Sprechstimme* employed in *Pierrot Lunaire*. *Sprechstimme* [known in English as speech-song] is a type of vocal delivery halfway between speech and singing: as well as rhythm, Schoenberg notates pitch down to the semitone, though this is customarily treated with great latitude [as it was under the composer's own direction].

Discussion points

– Do the pitch highpoints in the raps correspond to other musical elements, such as the ends of phrases or important rhythms?

– How close is the relationship between pitch and rhythm?

– In *G* above, were there any passages where the performing groups disagreed with the interpretation in the graphic score they were given?

Further study

There is a good deal of rap music readily available in commercial recordings. Similar in kind to the *Façade* music is *Sir John Betjeman's Varsity Rag* with music by J. Parker (Charisma 29). A corollary to *Sprechstimme* may be found in Rex Harrison's performance of *I've grown accustomed to her face* from *My Fair Lady*, or, indeed, in the dialect monologues of Stanley Holloway. Another kind of approximate pitching may be found in the talking-drum music from Africa, in which the drum imitates the tonal patterns of some African languages.

3 Copycat do→so

This activity is designed to develop an awareness of pitch relationships within the partial major scale do→so.

Procedure

A Get the students to sing back four one-bar phrases, which should use all the first five notes of a major scale, but no more. For example:

$\frac{4}{4}$ ♩ ♩ ♩ ♩	Students	♫ ♫ ♩ ♩	Students	♩ ♩ ♩ ♩	Students	♫ ♫ ♩	Students
d r m d	copy	m m r r m s	copy	m f s d	copy	m m r r d	copy

The students' repeats should come back without a gap, and it may be helpful to have someone tap out a steady beat. Try to design the one-bar melodies so they fit together into a four-bar phrase: this will help introduce the concept of phrasing.

B   Ask the students to identify how many different pitches were used in the exercise. It may be necessary to analyse the four melodies separately.

C   Sing the notes as a scale and ask the class which notes are closest together. The concept of tones and semitones could be introduced at this point.

D   Get each student to write or draw a vertical map of the five-note scale, using either arabic numbers, Tonic Solfa names (*do re mi fa so*) or pitch names (C D E F G), such as:

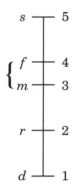

Make sure that smaller distance of the semitone — 3/4, *mi/fa* or E/F — is reflected in the map, or with a bracket. These maps could be compared to a diagram of a keyboard set on its side, vertically.

E   Repeat *A*, getting the students to follow the notes on their maps as they are sung. The first note of the first melody should be named in advance.

F   Repeat *A* with the students singing their answers in pitch numbers, solfa names or pitch names as appropriate.

G   Repeat *F*, using new melodies.

Variations and extensions

i) Echo game
Gather the students into a circle. Get one student to sing/play a note from the scale, and the next student to repeat it on the same beat of the bar, in a pattern such as

As this note is passed round the circle, the first student should send other single notes to follow it.

ii) Gather the students into a circle. Get one student to invent a one-bar melody drawn from the notes of the scale. The next student copies this without a break, the third student invents a new one-bar melody, which the fourth copies — and so on, without a break in the beat, round the circle. Every student should be given the chance both to invent and to copy: with an odd number of students, simply go twice round without a break; with an even number, go round two separate times, the second time beginning with the original second student.

38   *Pitch and Melody*

iii) Give each student or group of students a pitch from the five-note scale. Play or sing to the students some longer melodies, getting them to respond to the appearances of their allotted notes by some physical gesture, such as raising the hand or standing up. See if the class can sing the melody back, each student singing only the note allotted, like a set of human hand-bells.

iv) Divide the students into pairs or small groups and get them to work out the order of pitches in popular tunes which confine themselves to just these notes, such as *Oh when the saints* or Bob Dylan's *The times, they are a-changin'*.

Further study

Playing the partial scale *do→so* is covered in Units 2 and 3 of the instrumental workbooks which complement this book. Ensemble Piece No.1 confines itself to just this scale: the score can be found in the separate *Ensemble Scores* volume and the parts in Unit 3 of the workbooks.

Activity 4 expands on the work done here, introducing the pentatonic scale.

4 Copycat major pentatonic

This activity is designed to complement Activity 3, but using the major pentatonic scale (d r m s l), which it introduces.

Procedure

A   Revise the partial major scale (*do→so*) learnt in the previous activity.

B   Play/sing this scale to the students, followed by the major pentatonic scale (*do, re, mi, so, la*), getting them to identify where a pitch has been added and where one has been taken away.

C   Get the students to make new pitch maps, along the lines of:

Point out that the new scale pattern contains a leap of three semitones (a minor third), larger than any in the other scale. This should be reflected in the scale map.

D   Repeat the main procedure of Activity 3 (steps *E* and *F*), using melodies from the new scale.

E   Divide the students into pairs and get them to continue the copycat method, using the scale maps for reference. Make sure the students take turns at inventing and copying.

F   Demonstrate how the pitch maps can be extended to produced a three-line stave capable of being used to write down all the melodies heard so far:

Short 3-line stave

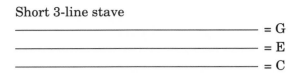

Sing/play some simple melodies using the pentatonic scale and get the students to transcribe the pitches by making dots on the lines or in the spaces. Examples of such melodies include:

Traditional Welsh: *Suo-gan*

Dvořák: *New World* Symphony (cor anglais solo from Largo)
(original key: D♭ major)

Grieg: *Morning Mood* from *Peer Gynt* (opening flute melody)
(original key: E major)

G   Repeat *E*, with each student in turn writing out in short-stave notation a pentatonic melody improvised by the other.

Variations and extensions

  i) Introduce two-bar melodies to stretch the students' memories.
 ii) Vary the time signatures used.
iii) Extend the scale to include the octave *do* (*do'*) and the lower *so* and *la* (*so'* and *la'*), for which these examples could be used:

Traditional Chinese: Boat Song

Traditional Scottish: *Auld Lang Syne*

iv) *Echo Game*

As i) in Activity 3, except that the pentatonic scale is used. This time, however, the echo should occur on the next beat of the bar and the student whose turn falls on the first beat of the bar (ie. students 1, 5, 9, 13 etc.) should present a new pitch. The result should be something like:

Further study

The latin-style Ensemble Piece No.2 uses the major pentatonic scale of C. The score can be found in the separate *Ensemble Scores* volume, and the parts in Unit 5 of the instrumental workbooks which complement this volume.

Pentatonic melodies may be found in Brian Brocklehurst's *Pentatonic Song Book* (Schott) and in Gaik See Chew's *Dragon Boat* (Chester). Use of the scale is characteristic of many Scottish folk-melodies, for instance *The Skye Boat Song*.

5 Question and answer

This activity is designed to develop skills in and awareness of melodic answering phrases.

Procedure

A   Revise the major pentatonic scale from the previous activity by singing up and down the scale, a note each in turn round a circle. (Try using the scale as a round: a four-part round with each part singing up and down the scale and coming in after two

notes quickly settles down into an alternation of the two chords)

B   It may be necessary to have a pulse-keeper during what follows. This could be a metronome, but if it is to be a student, that person needs to be chosen and prepared at this point.

C   Choose a leader who has to invent a one-bar melody using the pentatonic scale, which the remaining students must copy without a break. The process should be familiar from the copycat games played in the two previous activities, but it may be necessary for the leader to repeat the idea several times before the others can copy it exactly.

D   Once this melody has been established, get the leader to repeat it and the next student in the circle to invent an answering idea, again without a break.

E   Get the whole class to repeat the question and answer.

F   Repeat C–E as an unbroken six-bar phrase. Its structure should resemble this example:

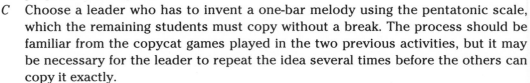

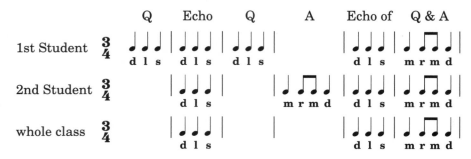

G   Repeat F with new students and new melodies. Ideally, this should be continued until every student has had a turn at both question and answer, but constraints of numbers and time may make this impossible.

H   Divide the class into pairs and get them to alternate question and answer roles. Some of the more successful ideas could be written down using the short-stave notation used in Activity 4.

Variations and extensions

i) Repeat G cumulatively, making each leader recap all the previous questions and answers before introducing the new question. The pattern of question and answer then becomes:

Students

1	Q^1		Q^1									
2				A^1								
3						Q^1	A^1	Q^2		Q^2		
4											A^2	
5/6												
Class	Q^1		Q^1	A^1			Q^2			Q^2	A^2	

Students

1/2/3/4										
5	Q^1	A^1	Q^2	A^2	Q^3		Q^3			
6								A^3		
Class						Q^3		Q^3	A^3	and so on . . .

In small groups the student who gave the first answer may follow as the second questioner, in which case the second student takes both lines 2 & 3 above, the third student 4 & 5 and so on. With large groups, however, the recapitulation procedure would rapidly become endless. (The cumulative process might be explained by an analogy with the chorus of *The 12 Days of Christmas*.)

ii) Repeat *G* using two-bar melodies for question and answer.

iii) To underline question-and-answer phrase structure, get the students to end every question melody on the *so* of the scale and every answer on the *do*.

iv) Try the activity using pitched percussion instruments, especially xylophones and glockenspiels, where bars can be removed to leave only the notes of the major pentatonic scale.

Discussion points

– If ideas were chosen for noting down in *H*, what factors led to the choice?

Further study

Further work on question-and-answer techniques can be found in the instrumental workbooks which complement this volume.

Call and response techniques are often found in the worksongs of the black slaves of the American plantations (see Activity 22 of *Structure and Form*).

6 Three-note turnarounds

This activity introduces and explores melodic extensions and development of short motifs.

Procedure

A Sing/play the tune *Suo-gan* (for music see under *F* of Activity 4).

B Get the class to repeat the tune and work out which notes of the pentatonic scale are being used and in what order:

$$\frac{4}{4} \quad d \ r \ m \ \mid \ r \ d \ r \ \mid \ d \ r \ m \ \mid \ r \ m \ d \ \parallel$$

C Explain the structure of this melody: four three-note patterns, each with the same rhythm; the primary motif in the first bar repeated exactly in the third; and the remaining bars (2 & 4) being different permutations of the notes of the primary motif.

D Sing/play to the class a different set of three notes from the pentatonic scale, such as:

$$\frac{4}{4} \quad d \ m \ s \ \mid$$

E Get the students to identify the three notes used in your motif and to list all the possible groupings of those three notes. Apart from the primary motif itself there should be five further related motifs. In the case of the example given in *D*, these additional permutations are: *s m d/m s d/d s m/s d m/m d s*.

F Get the class to sing through these new motifs.

G Get the class to choose three of the new motifs to follow the primary motif and form a four-bar melody.

H Divide the students into pairs to repeat steps *E–G*. Stress that the three notes chosen to form the primary motif should be three different notes and should contain *do*.

Variations and extensions

i) Using a primary motif such as *d m r*, explain how the permutations *r m d/m d r/r d m* are, respectively, the retrograde (backwards), inversion (upside-down) and retrograde inversion (backwards *and* upside down) of the primary motif.

ii) Experiment with a four-note primary motif: this increases the total of additional permutations to 23. [The total permutations of all five notes of the pentatonic scale is an even more impressive 120.]

iii) Experiment with different rhythms and metres.

iv) Expand the motifs by repetition to two bars' length, as in this example by Jean-Jacques Rousseau [better known as one of the French Encyclopédistes and author of *The Social Contract*]:

J. J. Rousseau

d r d r m   r   m   r d m   r   r   d r m d   d

r   m d r   m   r   d r m   d   r   m   r m r   d

v) Explore and invent melodies based on bell chimes, such as Big Ben's:

$$m\ d\ r\ s, \qquad s, r\ m\ d \qquad m\ r\ d\ s, \qquad s, r\ m\ d$$

Discussion points

– In *G* above, what criteria were used for selecting the motifs that would make up the four-bar tune?

Activities 7–12

AIMS

1 To develop further the concept of pitch scales, using the major scale, the minor pentatonic (*l, d r m s*) and natural minor scales.

2 To introduce the idea of melodic sequence.

3 To establish and consolidate skills in melodic phrasing and improvisation.

4 To explore further graphic notation.

7 Major connections (tetrachord)

This activity introduces the major scale, starting from the partial major scale (do→so) introduced in Activity 3.

Procedure

A Refer back to Activity 3, revising as necessary to get the students singing freely up and down the partial major scale (*do→so*).

B Get the students to sing up and down the *do→so* scale, marking the notes either side of the semitone (ie. *mi* and *fa*) with some physical gesture — clapping, tapping a foot etc.

C Once awareness of the position of the semitone is clear, get the students to sing up from do to so, repeat the final note as a new do and carry on upwards with a new *re*, *mi* and *fa*.

D Repeat this new scale without the doubled note in the middle, but with the correct Solfa names (if used): *do re mi fa so la ti do'*.

E Refer back to the *do→so* pitch maps used in Activity 3, and show that the new scale is, in effect, one pitch map on top of another.

F Show that the major scale consists of two tetrachords with an identical intervallic structure — tone, tone, semitone (*do→fa* of the pitch maps) — and that these tetrachords are separated by a tone (*fa/so* of the bottom tetrachord). [The word *tetrachord*, it could be pointed out, comes from the ancient Greek words for "four" and "string".]

G Get the students to produce new pitch maps covering the entire major scale, using either Solfa nomenclature (*do/d — do'/d'*) or pitch numbers (*1–1'*). As in Activities 3 and 4, care should be taken that the presence and position of semitones are reflected in the layout of the pitch maps.

H Get the students, using their maps, to work out the notes used by some well-known tunes, writing down the order in which they occur. The following examples show the ranges of the tunes and the first note in each case:

1. Tunes confined to the octave *do→do'*	Overall range	1st note
With a little help from my friends (Lennon and McCartney, from the *Sgt Pepper* album)	*do→do'*	*mi*
Troika from Prokofiev's suite *Lieutenant Kizhe*	*do→do'*	*so*
Brahms' Lullaby	*do→do'*	*mi*

2. Tunes extending down to lower *so,*		
Groovy kinda luv	*la,→la*	*do*
Signature tune to *East Enders*	*so,→la*	*do*
By the waters of Babylon	*so,→so*	*so,*
Beethoven's *Ode to Joy*	*so,→so*	*mi*
God save the Queen	*ti,→la*	*do*
Bob Marley's *One Love*	*so,→so*	*mi*
Rolling Stones' *As Tears go by*	*la,→la*	*do*

3. Tunes extending up beyond do'

Signature tune to *Neighbours**	*mi→la'*	*la*
Signature tune to *The Flintstones*	*do→re'*	*so*

*NB. This tune contains a note which is not part of the major scale. Which one is it?

Variations and extensions

i) Consider the other permutations of two tones and a semitone that make up different tetrachords: tone/semitone/tone, the basis of the minor scale (two are used in the natural minor scale to be explored in Activity 10); and semitone/tone/tone, the basis of the hypothetical Locrian mode.

ii) Make up new scales out of two different tetrachord patterns. Which sound the most interesting?

iii) Extend the three-line stave introduced under *F* of Activity 4 to five lines. Show how the major scale and pitch maps relate to this. If appropriate, introduce the treble clef sign.

8 Melodic riffs

This activity explores the effect of superimposing repeated melodic riffs.

Procedure

A   Revise the octave scale introduced in the previous activity.
B   Extend this scale downwards to the lower *so* (*so,*).
C   Working in a circle, get one student to invent a bass riff, drawing notes from the major scale in the range *so,→do'*, along the lines of:

do   do   so, la, ti,   do   do'

[At first, you may find it safer to use a bass riff of your own.]

D   Pass this riff round the circle, without any gaps in the rhythm, for which a pulse-keeper (or drum machine) may be necessary.
E   Select a student or small group of students to keep this bass riff going.
F   Over the bass riff, get the next student to invent a second riff, which is passed round the remainder of the circle. It is important that this new riff, and all the subsequent ones, should complement the existing texture both harmonically and rhythmically.
G   Select a student or small group of students to keep this second riff going.
H   Repeat *F* and *G* until a full texture is built up involving the whole class.

Variations and extensions

i) Use different time signatures or scales.
ii) Make a structured piece by using different riff groups at different stages, according to a pre-arranged pattern.

iii) Get the students to write down the pitches of some of the riffs, using the most advanced notation reached under Activity 7.

iv) If the treble clef was introduced under iii) of Activity 7, this might be a good place to introduce the bass clef. Get the students to write down the pitches of the bass riff(s) using it.

Further study

Activity 8 of *Structure and Form* deals with the 8-bar ground bass.

There are many examples of riff ostinatos, for instance on the xylophone in *We work the black seam together* from Sting's *The dream of the blue turtles* (A&M Dream 1), while bass riffs are a feature of the reggae style.

Ask students to bring in examples of the latest dance music, much of which will probably be riff-based.

9 Minor pentatonic excursions

This activity introduces the minor pentatonic scale and uses it for improvisation.

Procedure

A   Revise the major pentatonic scale learnt in Activity 4. Get the students to sing/play up the scale from *do* to *do'*: *do re mi so la do'*

B   Get the students to sing/play the same notes, but beginning on the lower *la* (*la,*) and ending on *la*: *la, do re mi so la*

C   Sing/play the two scales in alternation a few times.

D   Discuss how starting on la, alters the "feel" of the scale. Show how this is largely due to its opening with a minor third (la,/do).

E   Get the students to make a new pitch map for the scale, corresponding to those used in Activities 3 & 4:

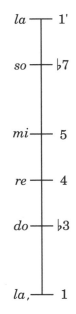

la	1'
so	♭7
mi	5
re	4
do	♭3
la,	1

Note that pitch maps using numbers will need to take some account of the relative flattening of 3 and 7, for example using ♭3 and ♭7 as above.

F   Using the new minor pentatonic scale, give the students one-bar phrases to echo, as in *A* of Activity 3. To emphasise the "minor" quality of the scale, it may be necessary to stress the note la.

G   Expand this using the copycat (as in ii of Activity 3) and question-and-answer (as in *C–F* of Activity 5) procedures.

Variations and extensions

i) Rehearse and perform Ensemble Piece No.5, which uses this scale The score can be found in the separate *Ensemble Scores* volume, and the parts in Unit 11 of the instrumental workbooks.

ii) Learn tunes using this scale, such as the negro spiritual *Didn't my Lord deliver Daniel* and the white spiritual *Poor wayfaring stranger*. The second of these forms the basis of Ensemble Piece No.4 (score in *Ensemble Scores*, parts Unit 9 of the workbooks).

Further study

Many blues tunes are based on this scale. The structure of the blues is dealt with in Activities 9 & 10 of *Structure and Form*. A third ensemble piece, No.6 (score in *Ensemble Scores* volume, parts in Unit 13 of the workbooks) also uses the scale.

10 Natural minor scale

This activity introduces the natural minor scale and links it to the major scale.

Procedure

A   Refer back to var.i) of Activity 7. Get the students to build a pitch map based on two tetrachords of tone/semitone/tone. Unlike the major scale, however, the last note of the first tetrachord must here become the first note of the second tetrachord, that is:

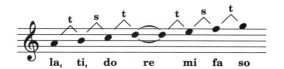

la,   ti,   do   re   mi   fa   so

B   Get the students to sing up this scale, making sure that the minor/flattened 6th and 7th notes are pitched accurately.

C   Repeat, marking the two pairs of notes a semitone apart with claps or taps:

D   Get the students to produce a definitive pitch map for the new scale, using either Solfa names or pitch numbers:

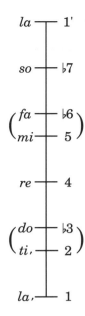

Note that with Solfa names it is customary to begin this scale on *la₁*, while with pitch numbers it will be necessary to mark in some way the flattening of 3, 6 & 7.

E   Get the students to sing the scale again twice in a row, beginning and ending the second time on the flattened third, in other words the two scales *la₁→la* and *do→do'*.

F   Point out and explain the relationship between these two scales, respectively the natural minor and major scales.

G   Get the students to write out the notes of the well-known Christmas carol *God rest you merry, Gentlemen*, using either Solfa names or pitch numbers (with provision for the flattened notes 3, 6 & 7):

God Rest Ye Merry, Gentlemen

(Traditional Carol)

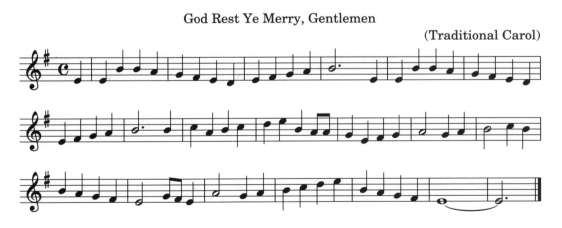

Variations and extensions

i)   Convert telephone numbers into tunes to sing. The numbers 1–8 become the notes of the natural minor scale, 0 equals the lower flattened seventh (*so₁*) and 9 is used for the upper second (*ti*).

ii) Get the students to transpose *God rest you merry, Gentlemen* by singing it from their transcriptions, but starting with a different pitch for *la₁*.

iii) Get the students to try and add some indications of rhythms and note values to the transcriptions produced under *G*.

iv) Repeat *G* with other tunes using this scale, for instance the Somerset folk-song *Farewell, Nancy*:

Fare - well my dear-est Nan-cy, since_ I must now_ leave you, Un -

to the salt_ seas I_ am_ bound for to go, But

let my long ab - sence be_ no trou - ble_ to you, For_

I shall re - turn in the Spring_ as you_ know.

Praetorius' round *Rise up, o Flame*:

Rise up, o Flame_____ by ___ thy_ light glow - ing

Show to us beau - ty,_ vi - sion _ and joy.

Axel F (the theme tune from the *Beverly Hills Cop* films) or the Israeli national anthem *Hatikvah*. Dave Brubeck's *Unsquare Dance* (see Activity 23 of *Rhythm and Metre*) is another, more complex example.

Further study

The natural minor scale is used further in Units 10 and 11 of the instrumental workbooks which complement this book.

11 Melodic extension: sequential motifs

This activity explores the sequential use of motifs as a means to construct and extend melodies.

Procedure

A   Present the students with examples of tunes made up of the sequential treatment of a primary motif, such as:

Wagner: *Tannhaüser: Pilgrim's Chorus*

Beethoven: Symphony No.5 (opening of 1st movement)

Mendelssohn: overture *Fingal's Cave* (opening)

B   Get the students to play/sing the examples wherever practicable.
C   Get the students to describe how the composer in each case has manipulated the primary motif to construct the theme.
D   Present the students with motifs along the lines of

(used either in the major or relative minor)

E   Get the students (individually or in small groups as appropriate) to develop a motif sequentially and produce a tune. It might be helpful to specify with each sample motif a scale within which the resulting tune must be confined.

F   Repeat *E* with the students inventing their own primary motifs.

G   Choose one of these resulting tunes to be played to the remainder of the class.

H   Get this remainder to identify:

      a) the type of scale being used

      b) the scale notes making up the primary motif

      c) the way this motif is developed

I   Repeat *G* and *H* as circumstances allow/dictate.

Variations and extensions

i) Play a recording of the first movement of Beethoven's Fifth Symphony, noting how much of the content relates to the primary motif.

ii) See whether students can think of any examples of tunes based on sequential repetition of primary motifs.

Discussion points

– Were there any places in the invented tunes where you wanted to change the intervals of the primary motif to make it fit? Why? [Compare the entry in b.7 of the Beethoven above.]

– Did your tunes ever need passages not based on the primary motif? Where and why?

– Can you really call the opening theme of the Beethoven Fifth Symphony a "tune", since it is split up amongst the instruments?

Further study

Other music based on sequential use of motifs includes the song *Do-re-mi* from Rodgers and Hammerstein's *The Sound of Music* and the Jamaican digging song *Imo Gal*, recorded on the album *Black Music of Two Worlds* (Folkways, FOL/FE 4602). It also lies at the base of the round *By the waters of Babylon*, used in Activity 7 of *Structure and Form*.

    The first movement of Mozart's Piano Trio in B flat, K.502 makes much use of a primary motif with the same shape as the last two examples under D above.

    More complex work on the use of sequences in melodic structure forms the basis of Activity 17 below.

12 Pitch cards

This activity is designed to develop the ability to improvise, using graphic symbols to suggest pitch relationships.

Preparation

This activity calls for instruments and several identical sets of graphic cards, such as:

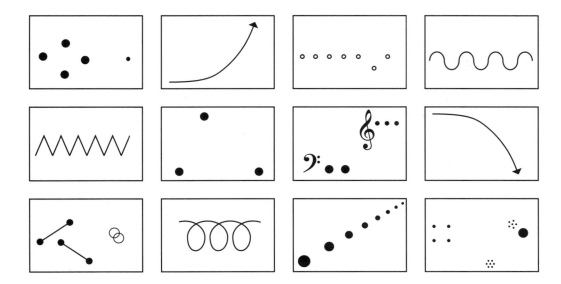

Each set should contain simple symbols, and you will require as many sets as there will be groups under *A* below.

Procedure

A Divide the students into small groups of about six each and give each group a set of graphic cards.

B Discuss with the class how the symbols might be interpreted. A range of interpretations should be encouraged.

C Get each group to prepare an instrumental and/or vocal piece based on some of the cards. The members of each group must discuss and decide:

    a) which instrument/voice each will use
    b) which cards to choose
    c) what order to use them in
    d) which way up to put each card
    e) how to interpret the various symbols
    f) what to call their piece

NB It may be advisable to divide the available instruments between the groups before embarking on *C*. Also, it may be easier for the students to decide on titles after they have heard their piece in rehearsal.

D Give each group enough time to assemble and rehearse its piece.

E Choose one group to perform its piece for the rest of the class.

F See if the others can work out which cards were used, in what order and which way up.

Variations and extensions

  i) Use cards with short-stave notations.

  ii) See what effect it has on the piece if the groups exchange instruments.

 iii) Let the students make up their own cards.

 iv) Get students to use single cards as the basis of an extended and developed improvisation, as opposed to merely interpreting the shapes of the symbols.

  v) The book of *Ensemble Scores* which accompanies this book contains three graphic scores for ensemble performance.

– Which cards suit a particular instrument or type of instrument? Why?
– Which symbols are the most ambiguous or the least clear and obvious? Is this a good thing or a bad thing? How could the ambiguous signs be made clearer and vice versa?
– How well did each piece live up to its title? Would a different title alter the way a particular piece is played?

Activities 13–18

AIMS

1 To develop further the concept of scale to include the melodic minor scale and Indian ragas.
2 To explore the ability of melodic shape and pitch movement to enhance the meaning of lyrics.
3 To develop further skills in phrasing and in the extension of melodies by means of sequences.
4 To explore pitch decoration.

13 Sharps up-flats down — the melodic minor

This activity introduces the melodic minor scale, connecting it with the natural minor scale.

Procedure

A Get the students to sing (at this stage without words) or play the following:

Sharp-en'd sixth and sev'nth go-ing up, but go-ing down they're flat-ten'd so it makes a smooth line. Me -

lo- dic mi- nor scales are diff-'rent go-ing up than when they are fall - ing down by step.

B   Get the students to put numbers under each note of this tune, using E=1 as a base. The opening should read: 6, 7, 1 1 1 2 ♭3 4 ♭3 2 1 ♭7, 5, etc.

C   Remind them of the natural minor scale discussed in Activity 10.

D   Ask them to identify which notes in the new tune do not belong to the natural minor scale.

E   Sing or play them the tune from *A* as it would be using only the notes of the natural minor scale [ie. with all Cs and Ds natural]. You could get the students to copy you.

F   Discuss why the tune sounds more melodic with the 6th and 7th notes raised on the way up and lowered on the way down.

G   Get the students to sing the tune from *A* again, this time with the words.

H   Divide the students into two groups and repeat *G* as a round. (The second group enters when the first group moves on to the second line.)

I   Get each student to draw a new pitch map for the scale (as in Activities 3, 4, 7, 9 & 10). There should be both ascending and descending versions.

Variations and extensions

i)   Get the students to try to memorise the explosive opening phrase from Beethoven's F minor Quartet, Op.95, which encapsulates the difference between the ascending and descending forms of the melodic minor scale:

Allegro con brio

ii) Get the students to work out the notes used in tunes based on the melodic minor scale, such as: the main theme of the slow movement of Tchaikovsky's Fourth Symphony; *Yesterday* from the Beatles' film *Help*! There are several tunes which contain only the descending form of the scale: the opening of Schubert's *Unfinished Symphony*; *Il vecchio castello* and *Bydlo* from Musorgsky's *Pictures from an exhibition*; the opening orchestral entry of Rakhmaninov's Second Piano Concerto; *Summertime* from Gershwin's *Porgy and Bess*.

Further study

The opening of the slow movement of the Beethoven Seventh Symphony, used in Activity 20 of *Timbre and Texture*, is also based on the melodic minor scale.

14 Introducing ragas

This activity introduces some melodic aspects of classical North Indian ragas.

Preparation

This activity calls for commercial recordings of *ragas*. One (for use in *A* and *B*) should be based, for ease of analysis, on one of the following pentatonic *ragas*:

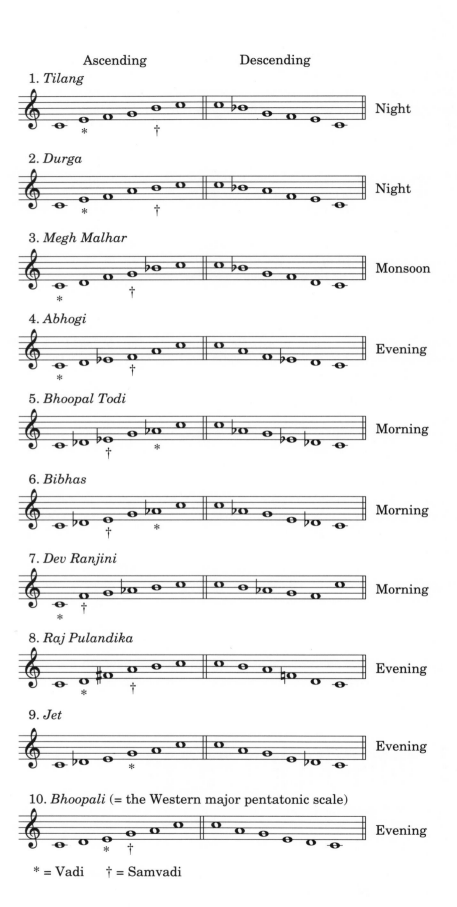

Pitch and Melody

Other useful seven-note *ragas* are:

1. *Skudh Bilanal* (= a Western major scale)

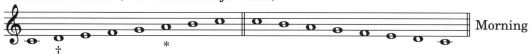

Morning

2. *Kafee* (= the Western Dorian mode)

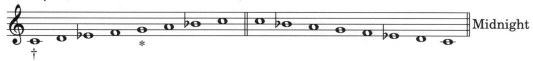

Midnight

3. *Bhairavi* (a popular *raga* appearing on many recordings)

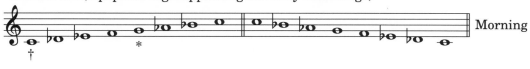

Morning

* = Vadi   † = Samvadi

Note that these *ragas* have been transcribed by the author into Western notation.

Procedure

A   Play the introductory section (*alap*) of any recorded *raga*. (Rhythmic aspects of the *alap* feature in Activity 6 of *Rhythm and Metre*.)

B   Play the recording a second time, having asked the students to make a note of any stylistic features to do with melody that occur to them. The sort of points that may emerge are:
  – the melody sounds improvised
  – one or two notes seem to be given prominence
  – the melody is elaborate, with principal notes brought out with inflections and decorations
  – drone accompaniment

C   Get the class to discuss their observations in detail. Some important aspects of *ragas* are given below. Draw attention to the points if they tie in with or explain a student observation.
  – Indian melodies are based on *ragas*. A *raga* consists of a series of 5–7 pitches, with an ascending (*aroh*) and descending (*avaroh*) form. Quite often these two forms differ both in the pitches used and even in the number of notes: in this respect they behave a bit like the melodic minor scale found in Activity 13.
  – Melodic improvisations are based round the chosen raga, ascending phrases using the *aroh* and descending ones the *avaroh*.
  – Each *raga* is derived from a parent scale. In North Indian music these are called *thaats* and there are 10 of them: in South Indian classical music, though, there are 72 of these parent scales, called *melakartas*.
  – Every *raga* has a prime note called a *vadi* and a secondary note called a *samvadi*. These are given particular prominence in melodic improvisation and are marked in the examples above.
  – *Ragas* are designed to convey a particular mood and character, and are meant for use at certain times of the day. The word *raga* comes from the Sanskrit *ranj*, which means "to colour with emotion".

- The *raga* system is an aural tradition, and Indian musicians do not use written notation systems. The pitches, however, do have names, and when these are written down they look not unlike our own Tonic Solfa system:

Western Solfa: *do*   *re*   *mi*   *fa*   *so*   *la*   *ti*   *do'*
Indian symbols: *sa*   *re*   *ga*   *ma*   *pa*   *da*   *ni*   *sa'*

As in Western systems there are semitones between some of these: re, ga, da and ni can be flattened, which is shown by underlining — *re*, *ga*, *da*, *ni*; similarly *ma* can be sharpened, which is shown by adding a vertical line above it — *m'a*. Unlike most Western melodies, though, Indian music can also use quarter-tones, dividing our 12-semitone octave into 22 quarter-tones, called *srutis*.

D   Get the class to sing, in both its ascending and descending forms, the pentatonic *raga* of your selected recording.

E   Play the recording.

F   Get the students to describe how the musicians are using the *raga*.

Variations and extensions

i) Try *C–F* with a seven-note *raga*.
ii) Activity 15 is a direct extension of Activity 14.

15 Basic improvisations around a raga

This activity follows on from Activity 14. It explores simple melodic improvisation using a pentatonic raga.

Procedure

A   Choose one of the pentatonic *ragas* given as examples in the previous activity, preferably one for which you have a recording. The examples here are based on the *Tilang raga*.

B   Get the students to sing up and down the raga in question, using the *sa-re* symbols and making sure to observe the differences between *aroh* and *avaroh* forms. In the case of the *Tilang* example, for instance, care should be taken to flatten *ni* on the way down, as follows:

C   Introduce an Indian time-cycle such as were used in Activity 6 of *Rhythm and Metre*. The following example uses the *Tal Char* cycle, whose 12 beats fit the six-note-up, six-note-down pattern of the raga:

D   Get the students to sing/play up and down the chosen *raga*, setting one note against each count of the *tala*, as in this example (starting at 6 o'clock position):

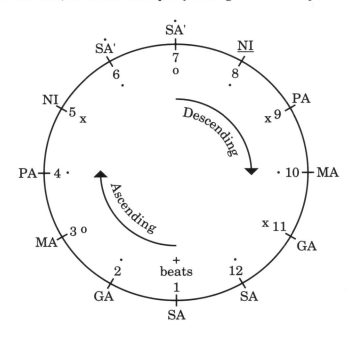

o = Khali beat (silent wave)
+ = Sam beat (clap)
x = Tali beats (click)
· = finger counts
(numbers = beats)

E   Repeat *D* with two pitches per count (ie. effectively in quavers) and then with four pitches per count (semiquavers).

F   Assign some students to sing/play a drone consisting of *sa* and *pa* (ie. a fifth).

G   Over this drone, get the remaining students in turn to improvise around the *raga*, making sure that the *aroh* and *avaroh* are used properly for ascending and descending phrases.

Variations and extensions

i)   Try *G* with pairs of students improvising simultaneously over the drone. The improvisers should be encouraged to use imitative or question-and-answer techniques.

ii) In descending phrases try sliding between <u>*ni*</u> and *pa*. Similarly, try decorating *vadi* (*ga*) and *samvadi* (*ni*) note with microtonal inflections.

iii) Explain how in Indian music the *Tilang raga* is intended for performance at night and has some associations with the fetching of water. Explore ways in which melodic improvisations could suggest a feeling of night or of water.

Further study

For more information on *ragas* the following works are recommended: Ram Avtar's *Theory of Indian Ragas* (Pankaj Publications), R. & J. Massey's *The Music of India* (Kahn and Averill) and N.A. Jairazbhoy's *The Ragas of North Indian Music* (Faber).

The folk-songs of India use the *raga* system more loosely. Some examples may be found in *Bengali Children's Songs* (ILEA).

An example of an improvisation using the *Tilang raga* may be found on Side 2 track 4 of Vol.1 of *Anthologie de la musique classique de l'Inde* (GREM 1508).

16 Melodic impressions

This activity is designed to explore the emotional effect of melody. Can melodic shapes suggest particular moods or emotions? Can melody heighten or colour the meaning of words?

Procedure

A Play the students some short vocal phrases, along the lines of the following examples, without any mention of the associated words:

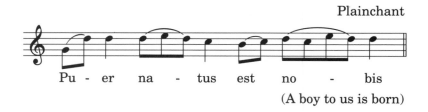

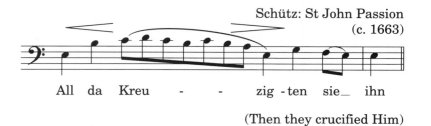

Moderato

J.S. Bach: Cantata No. 67
(1724)

Halt, - halt im Ge-dächt-nis Je - sum Christ

(Hold in remembrance of Jesus Christ)

Andante mesto

Verdi: Aida
(1870)

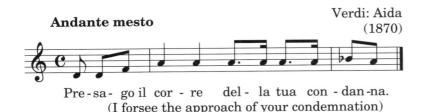

Pre-sa- go il cor - re del- la tua con-dan-na.

(I forsee the approach of your condemnation)

B   Get each student to make a note of the mood suggested by each phrase.

C   Compare and discuss the answers, still without reference to the texts involved.

D   Ask the students to try and match the melodic phrases used in *A* with their correct texts. Give them the texts and then the corresponding melodic phrases.

E   Discuss the answers. In the course of the discussion it is important to compare the moods noted by the students under *B* and *C* above with the actual emotional content of the text: this ought to show how far a melodic contour alone can suggest mood. The discussion could also touch on the expressive use of melisma, as in the Schütz example above, possibly making analogy with non-verbal means of vocal expression, such as sighs and groans.

F   Give the students the text of the *Agnus Dei* from the Mass: *Agnus Dei, qui tollis peccata mundi* [= Lamb of God, who takes away the sins of the world].

G   Get them to write a melody to match these words, choosing an appropriate key and scale.

H   Compare and discuss the results.

Variations and extensions

i) Listen to settings of the *Agnus Dei* by established composers, preferably using contrasting styles — Bach, Haydn, Dvořák, Janáček, Stravinsky.

ii) As an alternative to the *Agnus Dei* in *F–G*, use a descriptive poem such as *Icicles* from the *Cadbury's First Book of Children's Poetry* (Beaver), or possibly a Japanese *haiku*.

iii) Play recordings of songs with foreign texts and get the students to guess the subject matter. There are plenty of suitably graphic pieces in the song output of Schubert and Musorgsky, for instance.

iv) Extend the approach of iii) to non-vocal pieces, such as the Prelude to Wagner's *Tristan und Isolde* or Mendelssohn's Overture to *A Midsummer Night's Dream*.

v) Include pop songs where the melodic line clearly reflects the meaning of the words, as for instance in Legrand's *Windmills of my mind* and Stevie Wonder's *Lately* (especially the treatment of the word "Goodbye" in the chorus). Discuss how this heightening of the words is achieved.

Discussion points

– How far can melody alone create a mood? How far do other aspects of the music (rhythm, harmony, instrumentation etc.) contribute to the expressive effect?

Further study

For an interesting hypothesis on the meaning of melodic contours, see Deryck Cooke's influential *The Language of Music* (Oxford University Press).

17 Melodic extension: sequential phrases

This activity is designed as an extension to Activity 11, Sequential Motifs.

Procedure

A   Tell the students that you are going to play them a series of tunes and ask them to write down what feature they have in common.

B   Play some examples of melodies which make use of sequential repetition of whole phrases, such as:

Mozart: Symphony No.40 (opening of first movement)

Mozart: *Marriage of Figaro* (opening of *Se vuol ballare*)

C   Discuss the students' answers, establishing the fact that sequential phrases have been used.

D   Get the students individually or in pairs to compose a four-bar phrase and to extend this by sequential repetition. The repetition should start on a different note (most usually the second/supertonic) but keep to the same scale as the original phrase, so intervals may change from major to minor and vice versa. For instance:

E Get the students to alter the sequential repetition so that it exactly matches the original phrase, interval for interval. This will effectively change the key of the tune. Our example would become:

It might suit some of the tunes to alter the intervals in this way only towards the end of the repeated phrase, to effect a modulation — in the case of our example:

You might suggest this solution where appropriate to a particular student composition.

Variations and extensions

i) Try using phrases which begin sequentially, but end with a different contour, such as:

Schubert: *Lied der Mignon* (bb.7–14)

Handel: *Messiah* (from *But who may abide*)

ii) Compare the effects of motif (see Activity 11) and phrase when used sequentially in the formation of themes.

Further study

Clear examples of sequential themes of this kind include: the opening of Beethoven's *Waldstein* or *Appassionata* Sonatas, for instance, or of Schubert's little D major Violin Sonata, D.384, or of the finale of Sibelius' Violin Concerto, Strauss waltzes such as *The Blue Danube*, Gershwin's *A Foggy Day*, Vincent Youmans' *Tea for Two*.

The structural implications of sequences are dealt with in Activity 2 of *Structure and Form*, for which the present activity is a necessary preparation. Some melodic sequences are generated by underlying harmonic patterns: these are touched on in Activities 9 and 15 of *Harmony* and Activities 8–10 of *Structure and Form*.

18 Melodic decorations

This activity explores the use of ornaments and their effect on melodic lines.

Procedure

A   Play examples of pieces which make conspicuous use of ornaments — the highly ornamented music of the French *clavécinistes* (such as Couperin and Rameau), Chopin's Nocturne Op.9 No.2, the opening of Stravinsky's *Les Noces*, *Ballet of the unhatched chicks* and *Samuel Goldenberg and Schmuyle* from Musorgsky's *Pictures from an exhibition*, the Nocturne from Borodin's Second String Quartet, etc.

B   Repeat each example, getting the students to write down either in words or drawn shapes the way the melody has been decorated.

C   Collate and discuss the results of B. Where possible introduce the concepts of the commoner ornaments: *appoggiatura* (   ), a "leaning" note which takes half the value of the principal note (   ); *acciaccatura* (   ), a "crushed" note which is played as quickly as possible (   ) on the beat; trill (   ), in which the principal note is alternated rapidly with the note above (, or, in early music,   ); *mordent* (   ), in which the principal note is trilled briefly with the note above (, or, in early music,   ); *inverted mordent* (   ), where the principal note is trilled briefly with the note below   ; and *turn*, a twisting figure sometimes used as a decoration in its own right (, played   ) and sometimes acting as a springboard to get to a higher note (, played   ). With older or more experienced students, point out that there are many variants of the above and that realisations vary according to the attitude and education of the performer, no less than to the period and style of the music itself.

D   Get students individually or in RH/LH pairs to play the author's own *Decoration Blues*, which uses acciaccaturas, mordents and turns.

64   *Pitch and Melody*

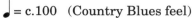

♩ = c.100   (Country Blues feel)

Variations and extensions

i) Play recordings of the decorative vocal styles of the Middle East, vocal music from Indian films, Indian ghazals and melismatic Western plainsong. Compare the techniques used.

ii) Get each student to produce a study composition focusing on one ornament.

Activities 19—24

AIMS

1 To develop further understanding of scales, introducing modal, chromatic and whole-tone patterns.
2 To explore counter-melodies.
3 To explore dissonant, chromatic and microtonal pitch movement.
4 To explore minor/major key changes.

19 Other scales

This activity is designed to introduce other scale patterns.

Preparation

This activity calls for commercial recordings of plainsong or early polyphony (*A*), as well as other music based on the Dorian, Phrygian, Lydian or Mixolydian modes, both folk/pop (*D* and *E*) and jazz/classical (*F* and *G*). It is also important to have recorded examples of music using any of the scale patterns you may wish to mention from vars.i) — iii).

Procedure

A Give the students a brief, simplified account of the history and significance of the system of church modes. Mention that the major/minor key system, on which nearly all music of the last 300–400 years is based, developed out of, and superseded, modes. It would be helpful to introduce or illustrate your account with a recording of plainsong or early polyphony.

B Explain the content of the various modes. This is probably still best done by imagining (or indeed playing) scales that use only the white notes of a keyboard instrument. The four principal church plainsong modes were as follows (solfa names are given in brackets):

D→D′	[*re*→*re*']	Dorian
E→E′	[*mi*→*mi*']	Phrygian
F→F′	[*fa*→*fa*']	Lydian
G→G′	[*so*→*so*']	Mixolydian

Two further modes were added later. They do not strictly belong to plainsong, but were suggested by a theorist in 1547 to reflect recent developments in music. They are:

C→C′	[*do*→*do*']	Ionian
A→A′	[*la*→*la*']	Aeolian

These are, of course, the major and natural minor scales, respectively, and their appearance in that book of 1547 is almost like a registration of their birth.

C   Get the students to work out the order of tones and semitones used in each of these modes.

D   Explain that modes, or at least traces of the commoner ones, still survive in folk music and folk-derived pop. The commonest are the Dorian mode (Simon and Garfunkel's *Scarborough Fair*, Lennon and McCartney's *Eleanor Rigby*, the verse from Sting's *We work the black seam together* and *Greensleeves*) and the Mixolydian (*The Rambling Sailor* and the Irish jig *Tatter Jack Walsh*).

E   Play recorded examples of this sort of music.

F   Explain that, similarly, modal scale patterns are used extensively by jazz musicians in improvisation. They are also used not infrequently by composers of classical music, particularly when they are looking for an archaic effect (eg. Beethoven's use of the Lydian mode in the slow movement of the A minor Quartet, Op.132) or basing music on folksong (eg. Vaughan Williams).

G   Play recorded examples of this kind of music.

H   Get each student to chose a mode and produce a melody using it.

Variations and extensions

i) Introduce the wholetone scale, which, as its name implies, consists of nothing but whole tones. Because all the intervals are the same, the scale is very distinctive, though it has very little sense of "direction" or of "home". This sense of being in "limbo" can give rise to very colourful effects, nowhere better than in the music of Debussy, for instance *Voiles* from the First Book of Preludes for piano. (Notice how the sustaining pedal of the piano can make the sounds overlap, producing a very atmospheric effect.) Play a recorded example of music using this scale.

ii) Introduce the harmonic minor scale, in which the sixth note of the scale is flattened but the seventh raised. (This is because the subdominant chord [IV] wants a minor third but the dominant chord [V] a major third — hence the name "harmonic".) The enlarged interval between the 6th and 7th notes (an augmented second) is a very characteristic one, much used in melodies of eastern European, middle eastern and even far eastern music. It is consequently much used in Western music which tries to imitate such sounds: the "oriental" music so beloved of Russian composers of the 19th century; the Hungarian/gipsy music with which Brahms and Liszt so often let their hair down; the music of Moorish Spain and North Africa, which became something of an obsession of the French in the late 19th and early 20th centuries, and so on. Play a recorded example of music using this scale.

iii) Mention other scale patterns developed and used by individual composers: Messiaen's *Modes of limited transposition*, derived from the idea of Indian ragas; Harry Partch's scale patterns using quarter-tones; Hauer's *Tropes* (a form of 12-note music that grew up beside Schoenberg's serial technique); even Rimsky-Korsakov's octotonic scale, which is made up of tones and semitones in alternation — C D E♭ F G♭ A♭ A B C. Play recorded examples of music derived from these scales.

iv) Get the students to explore a selection of these modes/scales, using the copycat, question-and-answer and echo techniques from Activities 3–5.

v) Get the students individually to invent a scale and compose a melody based on it. Since the established scales and modes mentioned above have exhausted so many possibilities, students could use five- or six-note scales. It might be interesting to ask the students to give their scale and melody a name.

vi) Make up random five-note scale patterns by taking five glass bottles and filling them with different quantities of water.

Further study

Ensemble Pieces No.8 and 9 make use, respectively, of the Mixolydian and Dorian modes. The scores can be found in the separate *Ensemble Scores* volume and the parts in Units 17 and 19 of the instrumental workbooks which complement this volume.

Thai classical music makes use of a scale pattern in which each interval is more or less equal: unlike the whole-tone scale, however, it splits the octave into seven, not six divisions.

20 Counter-melodies

This activity introduces the idea of a counter-melody in the form of a descant to a well-known tune.

Procedure

A   Divide the class into pairs.

B   Select a well-known tune, which is suitable for the addition of a descant counter-melody. A simple folksong or carol would be ideal.

C   Identify the type of scale used by the chosen tune, and, if necessary, revise this.

D   Get each pair to try to add a second, descant part to the principal melody, using exactly the same rhythms. The descant should keep in parallel with the principal melody, that is its notes should keep a set interval away, though the interval will of course change from major to minor and vice versa, depending on whereabouts in the scale any given note lies. Encourage the students to try out various intervals for this purpose and choose the most pleasing.

E   Get the students to compare and evaluate the results. Which were the most and which the least pleasing intervals to use? At an appropriate point in the discussion, explain the changing attitude to various parallel intervals throughout musical history. Parallel fourths and fifths were the first kind of harmonisation that appeared in Western music, in a style known as *organum* that was in use from the 9th to the 12th century:

from the *Schola Enchiriadis* (c.880)

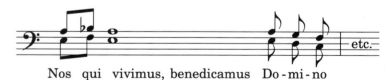

Nos   qui   vivimus,   benedicamus   Do - mi - no

Tu   Pa - tris   sem - pi - ter - nus   es   Fi - li - us.

The style was gradually replaced by more complex polyphony, until by the 16th century parallel fifths, for instance, were effectively prohibited, not to return until the late 19th century. Instead, parallel movement was nearly always in thirds or sixths, as, for instance:

Corelli: Trio Sonata, Op.3 No.4 (opening of Adagio)

[There are, incidentally, many examples of melodies in thirds in popular music. The Beatles used the device several times, for instance in *Two of Us* from the album *Let it Be*; another example is the Everly Brothers' *All I have to do is dream*.]

F Repeat *D*, with the descants now moving throughout in contrary rather than parallel motion.
G Get the students to perform and discuss the results of *F*.

Variations and extensions

i) Try creating a descant which moves in contrary motion *and* has contrasting rhythmic movement.
ii) Try creating the best possible descant by changing from parallel to contrary movement and from parallel to contrasting rhythms, as most appropriate to the principal melody.
iii) Play the melody pairs from ii) over the original harmony of the principal melody. How many descants still work?
iv) Play one after another the principal melody and all the successful candidates from iii), each over the original harmony. Are any of the descants better/more interesting than the principal melody? Why?

Discussion points

– Was it easier to produce descants in parallel motion, contrary motion or a combination of the two?

Further study

There are many examples in musical literature of the use of counter-melodies. Some of the clearest, perhaps, can be found in Baroque trio sonatas, such as those by Corelli and Handel; vocal duos, such as the Italian Duos by Handel or *Lieder* for two voices by Schumann, Brahms, etc.; or instrumental duos such as the 44 for two violins by Bartók. For old-fashioned descants *per se* there are many instances amongst hymns and carols, but for an off-beat example try the so-called "piccolo variation" from a Sousa march such as *The Stars and Stripes Forever*.

21 One small step and a leap

This activity is designed to explore chromatic inflections.

Procedure

A Divide the students into three equal groups.

B Get the students to sing up and down the first five notes of the minor scale.

C Assign the tonic, mediant and dominant of this scale (the 1st 3rd and 5th notes) one each to the three groups.

D Get the first group to sing:
  a) its note
  b) this note, the semitone above, and the note again
  c) the note, the semitone below, and the note again.

Thus:

E Repeat for the second group, and then the third.

F Devise (with or without student suggestions) hand signals to denote the inflections b) and c) above, plus another two to signify starting and stopping.

G Choose a student to act as conductor.

H Get this conductor to direct an improvised piece, bringing the groups in with their note and taking them out again, as well as indicating the use of semitone inflections according to the signals devised in *F*.

I Repeat with other conductors, as time allows.

J Divide the students into smaller groups (of at least four) to explore the possibilities of these ideas and to compose a short study with the title *One small step and a leap*.

K Perform and discuss the resulting pieces.

Variations and extensions

i) Compare the effect of using pitch benders on synthesisers.

ii) Play (if possible in a recording) the Dirge from Britten's *Serenade for tenor, horn and strings*:

This ae nighte, This ae nighte, e - ve - ry nighte and alle,

Fire and fleet and can-dle lighte, and Christe re-ceive thy saule.

Get the students to compare the technique used here to their own pieces.

iii) Activity 22 following is effectively an extension of this one.

22 Chromatic inflections

This activity explores the effect of chromatic inflection on the character of melodies.

Procedure

A   Get the students to sing up and down the first five notes of the minor scale.

B   Repeat with the intervening chromatic steps: a flattened second and a raised third and fourth. If necessary, the previous activity (21) may be revised first: the "small steps" used there include all the notes of the tonic-dominant chromatic scale except the perfect fourth, which should be familiar enough from the ordinary minor scale.

C   Devise a numerical pitch map of the new scale, such as:

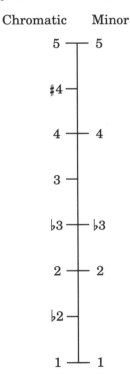

and then get the students to repeat the scale.

D   Get the students (individually or in pairs) to make up 4- or 8-bar melodies using the minor scale, occasionally adding notes from the new scale to fill in and colour the melodic line.

E   Play the results of *D* in turn to the class, asking the students to try to write down the order of the notes using numbers.

F   Discuss the characters of the various tunes. What part do the chromatic notes play?

G   Play some extracts from melodies which use chromatic notes, such as:

Grieg: *In the hall of the Mountain King* from *Peer Gynt*

Alla marcia e molto marcato

Beethoven: *Für Elise*

Beethoven: Minuet, WoO 10 No.2

Traditional Greek: Kalamata Dance

Gershwin: *It ain't necessarily so* from *Porgy and Bess*

Moderato scherzoso

For more examples, see under *Further study* below.

H   Discuss the character of these melodies, as under *F*. [You might get the students to try writing down the notes of some of the simpler melodies, as under *E*.]

Variations and extensions

i) Get the students (individually or in small groups) to prepare a composition based on a chromatic melody. You could set a title such as *The Snake* or *The Spiral Staircase*, or leave the title up to the composers.

ii) Compare the effect of falling and rising chromatic bass lines, such as:

Purcell: *When I am laid in earth* from *Dido and Aeneas*

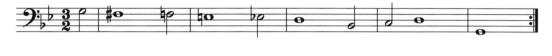

The last is characteristic of a 12-bar blues bass line, particularly for bars 11/12.

iii) Play recordings of appropriate Indian *raga*-based music and get the students to note the effect of chromatic and microtonal inflections. Here is a table showing Indian semitones and microtones:

Western Notes	C	C♯ or D♭	D	D♯ or E♭	E	F	F♯	G	G♯ or A♭	A	A♯ or B♭	B
Indian Notes (*swaras*)	SA	RE♭	RE	GA♭	GA	MA	MA♯	PA	DHA♭	DHA	NI♭	NI
Indian Microtones (*srutis*)	1, 2	3, 4	5, 6	7	8, 9	10	11, 12, 13	14	15, 16	17, 18, 19	20	21, 22
Names of Microtones		(1) Tivra; (2) Kumadvati; (3) Manda; (4) Chandovati	(5) Dayavati; (6) Ranjini; (7) Raktika		(8) Rudri; (9) Krodhi		(10) Vajrika; (11) Prasarini; (12) Priti; (13) Marjani		(14) Kshiti; (15) Rakta; (16) Sandipini; (17) Alapini	(18) Madanti; (19) Rohini; (20) Ramya		(21) Ugra; (22) Kshobini

Further study

There is no lack of music with chromatic inflections. The following melodies might be mentioned: themes from *The Third Man* and *The Pink Panther*; *Maria* from Bernstein's *West Side Story*; Scott Joplin's *Entertainer*; *Nuages* by Django Reinhardt; the Christmas classic *I'm dreamin' of a white Christmas*; the main woodwind and brass theme from *Mars* from Holst's suite *The Planets*; the main horn theme from Richard Strauss' *Till Eulenspiegel*; and the main theme from the first *Kyrie* from Bach's B minor Mass. The following might also be useful as short pieces permeated with chromaticism: the A minor Prelude and Fugue from Book II of Bach's 48; Chopin's Study in A minor, Op.10 No.2; Rimsky-Korsakov's *Flight of the bumble bee*; and *Mars* and *Uranus*, again from Holst's suite *The Planets*.

23 12-note rows

This activity explores the chromatic scale and in particular the construction of 12-note rows in a serial manner.

Procedure

A   Get the students to sing/play up and down a complete one-octave chromatic scale. Use the previous activity (22) for revision as necessary.

B   Get the students to fashion a three-note motif from the notes of one of the following chords:

For instance, this motif might be formed from the first chord:

C   As a class, work out the various permutations of the chosen motif. In the case of our example these would be:

– retrograde (backwards)

– inversion (upside down)

– retrograde inversion (upside down and backwards)

Note that when manipulating rows in this way, it is customary for every note to have its own accidental, whether sharp, flat or natural.

D   Get the class to transpose their four three-note motifs so that, between them, the Prime (P), Retrograde (R), Inversion (I) and Retrograde Inversion (RI) provide the 12 pitches of a chromatic scale. The motifs of our example could be transposed to produce the following row:

Any Prime drawn from the chords under *B* above will generate a row of this kind, provided the correct transpositions are found.

E   Get the students to sing/play the note row.

F   Experiment with the order of the motifs to obtain the most effective row.

G   Add rhythms to these pitches.

H   Get the students to invent their own 12-note rows using the same procedure.

Variations and extensions

i) Apply the principles of inversion, retrograde and retrograde inversion to the complete 12-note rows.

ii) Use the 12-note rows as canons — see Activity 6 of *Structure and Form* for work on canons.

iii) Make a piece out of the following row, giving the note-pairs (each forming a different interval) to six different players:

iv) Play, discuss and/or analyse recordings of serial music. See below for examples.

Discussion points

– Is it better to see the row as a series of 12 notes or as a series of 11 intervals?

Further study

There is no lack of serial music in published or recorded form. Its purest, most crystal-line manifestation is probably to be found in the later music of Webern (from Op.21 onwards: up to Op.16 is not serial), and particularly in the Quartet (for tenor saxophone, clarinet, violin and piano), Op.22 (see LAM 100), the Concerto, Op.24, the Piano Variations, Op.27, and the String Quartet, Op.28. The tone-rows used in these four works are as follows:

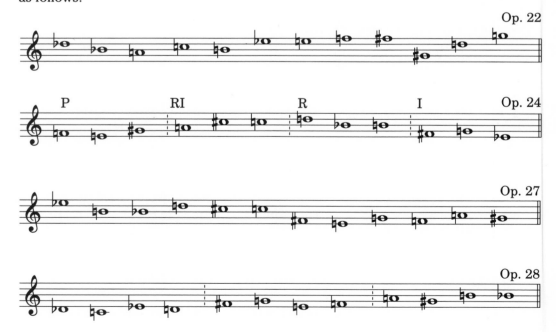

By contrast, in such a work as the Fourth String Quartet of Schoenberg it is possible to see music that makes exactly the same sort of gestures one might find in a tonal work of previous generations, but with pitches derived from serial procedures. Still less obvious serialism is to be found in such a work as Berg's Violin Concerto (see LAM 103), where the mathematical rule of the 12-note row is frequently bent for musical considerations.

Some composers have used 12-note themes in non-serial "tonal" works: Britten and (in his later period) Shostakovich both had leanings in this way. On the other hand Bartók (particularly in his middle period) used all the motivic manipulation characteristic of Webernian serialism, without using 12-note composition as such except by accident.

24 Minor→major transformations

This activity explores key changes from minor to major.

Preparation

Some work on phrase structures is necessary before this activity is attempted: see Activities 2 and 3 of *Structure and Form*. An understanding of imperfect and perfect cadences is also assumed: see Activity 7 of *Harmony*. Even where both subjects have already been covered, some revision would be advisable.

Procedure

A   Revise the melodic minor scale (Activity 13 above).

B   Get the students (working individually or in pairs) to invent two 8-bar phrases using the scale. The second phrase must end with an imperfect cadence; but it would also be appropriate for the first phrase to end with a perfect cadence, and for the opening of the second phrase to echo that of the first. Along the lines of:

C   Get the students to write these two phrases out again, this time in the tonic major, raising the 3rd, 6th and 7th of the scale where necessary. In the case of the above example:

D   Perform the results of this process as 32-bar themes modulating from minor to major.

E   Get the students to take the original two phrases in the minor and add two new 8-bar phrases in the major. This time the major phrases should contrast with the minor ones and the last phrase should end with a perfect cadence. As for instance:

F   Get each composer (pair) to play both forms of the 32-bar melody (the *D* form and the *E* form).

G   Compare and discuss the results.

Variations and extensions

i)   Play Ensemble Piece No.7, taken from Praetorius: the score can be found in the separate *Ensemble Scores* volume parts in Unit 15 of the instrumental workbooks. Analyse the changes of key.

ii) Play recordings of other melodies or short pieces which move from major to tonic minor or vice versa. Examples include the Pet Shop Boys' *In Suburbia*, Lennon and McCartney's *I'll be back*, the second movement of Beethoven's Piano Trio in E♭, Op.70 No.2 , Brahms' Fifth Hungarian Dance, Grieg's Waltz, Op.12 No.2, and Dvořák's famous *Humoresque*. Discuss the effects of the change.

iii) If one of the student themes contains, like the example above, many repetitions at the same pitch of a single motif, show the class the effect of playing the whole theme in the minor, just slipping briefly into the major for one of the immediate repetitions of the motif (in the above example this would involve playing the whole 32 bars in the minor, switching to the major for b.3 & 4 or b.11 & 12 or b.19 & 20 or b.27 & 28).

iv) Repeat the procedure of *F*, but use the relative rather than the tonic major. Some care will need to be taken over the join between the minor half and its major counterpart. One solution is a pivot: the dominant (5th) of a minor is the mediant (3rd) of the major; in other words a first half in G minor could end on the note D, which could open the second half as the third of the scale of B♭ major. But the two keys could be melodically linked just as easily by a couple of notes added as an upbeat. A good example of a tune modulating from minor to relative major is Paul McCartney's *Another Day*. In the famous Rondo *alla turca* from Mozart's Piano Sonata in A, K.331, the main theme begins and ends in A minor but modulates in the middle to the relative major, C: this theme, incidentally, is immediately followed by a section in the tonic major (A major), which modulates briefly into its own relative minor, F sharp minor.

v)   Experiment with changing major melodies into minor ones. A good example to use is Stephen Foster's *Old Folks at Home* ("Way down upon the Swanee river").

Discussion points

- How far does a change of key from minor to major, or vice versa, affect the mood of a piece?
- Was the version of the theme used at iii) better than the original, or just different?

Harmony

CONTENTS

81

Activities 1–6

AIMS

1 To explore drones.
2 To explore links between scales and chords.
3 To introduce and explore the triad (major and minor) and simple I–VI chord progressions.
4 To compare and contrast the effect on triads of close- and wide-spacing, sustaining and arpeggiation.

1 Drones

This activity introduces the drone, one of the earliest forms of harmonic accompaniment.

Preparation

This activity calls for three xylophones (or similar), each with one of the following notes:

Chime bars or three bars extracted from a single instrument would do as well.

Procedure

A Working in a circle, give one student the lower A instrument, the next in the circle the higher A and the next the E.

B Get the first student to play the note on the instrument provided, then sing it, holding the note (see *D* and *E* below).

C Repeat *B* with the second and third students.

D Get the fourth student to sing the same note as the first student, who may stop singing at this point.

E Repeat *D*, with the fifth student copying the second student, the sixth the third.

F Continue right round the circle.

G Repeat *B–F* until the exercise can be done quickly and without instruments.

H Get all the students to sing their allotted notes simultaneously and to hold the resulting drone indefinitely. With larger classes, breathing will be naturally staggered so that holding notes should be no problem for the group as a whole; but with smaller numbers, instruments may have to be used to help continuity.

I Repeat *H*, but get each student in turn to improvise a little inflection to the note, for instance moving to the semitone above or below. The other students should all keep to their pitches until their turn comes.

J Once the drone is well established, sing/play over it a suitable tune such as the spiritual *Swing Low*. This could be recorded, and the play-back discussed.

Variations and extensions

i) Divide the students into smaller groups to experiment with their own drones. Encourage them to try other intervals for the drone. They should then add a melody over their chosen drone.

ii) Sing the notes of the main activity

as though they were strings being plucked. Compare this sound to that of an Indian tambura. A similar effect may be produced on a guitar by retuning the strings as follows:

strings:	6	5	4	3	2	1
pitches:	E	A	E	A	A	E

(This involves retuning the 3rd and 4th strings up a tone: to avoid the risk of damage, it might be safer to compromise and retune the strings a semitone lower than shown.)

Discussion points

– Why are the tonic, octave tonic and dominant notes the most common drones?

Further study

There is a good deal of music involving the use of drones. European folk-music employing bagpipes or the hurdy-gurdy cannot escape its sound; and these instruments are sometimes imitated in classical music, for instance by Haydn in the opening of the finale to Symphony No.104, or by Schubert in the song *Der Leiermann* [=the hurdy-gurdy man] which closes the song cycle *Winterreise*.

Much north Indian *raga*-based music has a drone accompaniment provided by a tanpura, while more popular forms of Indian music employ a harmonium for this purpose.

The musette, originally the name of a form of gentrified bagpipe popular at the French court, is the name of a French dance form employing a drone and once used as the "trio" section of a gavotte: it was occasionally revived by later composers for archaic effect — in Grieg's *Holberg Suite*, Prokofiev's Classical Symphony, and Schoenberg's Suite for Piano, Op.25.

An interesting comparison to *I* above is provided by Stockhausen's vocal work *Stimmung*, which is a piece built round a single chord lasting up to an hour.

2 Triad sustain

This activity introduces the major and minor triads and shows their relation to scales.

Procedure

A   Get the students to sing up the first five notes of the major scale to the numbers 1, 2, 3 etc. If necessary, first revise Activity 3 of *Pitch and Melody* which introduces this partial scale.

B   Repeat, missing out the second and fourth notes. This will leave just: *one, three* and *five*.

C   Divide the class into three (geographically or alphabetically) and assign the three notes, one to each group.

D   Get the students to sing their allotted notes, and make sure that the resulting triad is "in tune". If the notes are still sung to the numbers *one, three* and *five*, it might help emphasise the link between scale and triad.

E   Form the students into a circle.

F   Get one student to sing/play and hold the first note, the next student in the circle the third note, the next student the fifth note, the next student the first note again. Where the triad is being sung, xylophones or chime bars may be necessary or helpful for pitching.

G   Continue round the circle, each student taking up the first, third or fifth note in succession. The triads should be in close formation, so broken male voices may have to form a separate, lower triad.

H   Repeat *A–G* with the first five notes of the minor scale. The various minor scales are dealt with in Activities 10, 13 and 19 of *Pitch and Melody*, but the first five notes are, of course, the same in all of them. Where the students are singing numbers to the three pitches of the triad, it might be useful to mark the flattening of the third by using a different word, for instance "down" or "flat".

I   Repeat *C–D* to a slow beat, getting the students to alternate four beats of sustained major triad with four beats of silence.

J   Repeat *I* with the minor triad.

K   Repeat *I–J* in the pattern: major triad — silence — minor triad — silence — major triad etc.

L   Divide the students into small groups to explore the effects of major and minor triads and to produce a short composition based on them.

Variations and extensions

i)   Get the students to sing the triad as at I, but as an off-beat quaver. Alternate major and minor every four beats, in the pattern:

ii) See how long the students can hold the triad by repeating I and increasing the sustaining time: 8 beats of note, 4 beats of silence; 12 beats of note, 4 of silence etc.

iii) The following activity (3) is designed to extend the present one by introducing the idea of arpeggiation.

Further study

Ensemble Piece No.1 uses only one chord (triad of C major). The score can be found in the separate *Ensemble Scores* volume and the parts in Unit 3 of the instrumental workbooks.

A number of pieces make significant use of sustained triads: the entire Prelude to Wagner's *Das Rheingold* is built on a chord of E flat major and the entire *Toccata* which opens Monteverdi's opera *Orfeo* is built on a chord of D major. There are similar minor triads opening *Shine on you crazy diamond* from Pink Floyd's album *Wish you were here* and closing the last movement of Shostakovich's Fourth Symphony.

Stockhausen's *Stimmung*, mentioned at the end of the previous activity, is based on a slightly more complex chord than a triad:

but this chord is sustained throughout the entire piece. Cf. Ligeti's works employing "micropolyphony".

Dramatic alternations of major and minor triads may be found in the introduction to Richard Strauss' *Also sprach Zarathustra* and in the finale of Mahler's Sixth Symphony.

3 Broken triads

This activity is designed to explore arpeggiation of the triads introduced by the previous activity.

Procedure

A Revise Activity 2 as necessary.
B Repeat *E–G* of Activity 2, but without sustaining any of the notes. The result should be broken triads.
C Introduce and briefly explain the terms "broken triad/chord".
D Repeat *B*, alternating major and minor triads.
E Divide the class into small groups.
F Get each group to experiment with broken triads: encourage them to try different orderings of notes and to extend the triad into the upper and lower octaves.
G Divide the class into four groups.
H Perform the following round based on a broken chord. The groups should enter at four-bar intervals:

Broken chord round - groups enter every four bars

Triplet minim and crotchet patterns could be included if appropriate

Variations and extensions

Get the students, in their small groups (as at *E*), to make up rounds based on a broken triad.

Further study

The techniques required for the construction of rounds in general are dealt with in the activities devoted to two- and three-part canons, Activities 6 and 7 of *Structure and Form*.

There are a number of pieces based on broken chords. In some minimalist music (for instance Terry Riley's *In C* and Philip Glass's *Glassworks*) the harmonies change very slowly, whereas the first Prelude from Bach's 48 Preludes and Fugues, and Chopin's Studies in C major (Op.10 No.1), A flat major (Op.25 No.1) and C minor (Op.25 No.12) all use more quickly-changing harmonies.

Numberless themes begin with broken chords, some of the most prominent being the first movement of Beethoven's *Eroica* Symphony and the last movement of his Violin Concerto, the opening of *Mendelssohn's* Octet and the *Dance of the Knights* from Prokofiev's *Romeo and Juliet*. The many examples in popular idioms include the introduction to Stevie Wonder's *Sir Duke*, Glenn Miller's *In the Mood* and Irving Berlin's song *Puttin' on the Ritz*. Shostakovich based the A major Fugue from his 24 Preludes and Fugues on a subject entirely made up of a single broken chord, to say nothing of the countless classical and preclassical uses of the so-called "Mannheim Skyrocket".

4 Spacing triads

This activity explores different spacings of triads and the effects of close-position triads in different registers.

Preparation

This activity calls for keyboards and/or guitars.

Procedure

A Revise Activity 2.

B Explain that the triads used in that activity were in close position; that is, the 1st, 3rd and 5th notes of the scale were the closest together they could be, occupying their proper scale positions. But the notes of a triad can be used in any order and in any register, with large or small gaps between.

C Play examples of open-position C major triads.

D Explain how the description "root position" is used for any triad with its name note (ie. C in the case of a triad of C major/minor) at the bottom; the positioning of the other two notes, provided they are above the keynote, makes no difference whatso-ever to the use of the term.

E Play a variety of root-position C major triads.

F Get the students, individually or in pairs (as instrument availability permits), to explore the effect of different spacings of a C major triad in root position.

G   Ask each student/group to produce the three most interesting examples.

H   Get the students/groups to explore the effect of using close-position triads in different registers.

I   Divide the class into slightly larger groups.

J   Get each group to produce a piece made up of the triad formations explored in *F* and *H*.

Variations and extensions

i)   Get the students to suggest the best spacing of a root-position C major triad for specific voices: high (soprano), high-middle (alto) and low-middle (tenor). Check these positions, using singers of the appropriate voices.

ii) Repeat *F–G* without restricting the exploration to root-position triads. Explain that these forms are called "inversions" of the triad; identify the first and second inversions where appropriate.

iii) Experiment with 4-note chords, doubling one of the notes of the triad in a different register. How does this affect the sound of the triad?

iv) Widen the scope of the pieces called for in *J* by allowing any of the following: triads in other than root-position; C minor triad; triads other than C major or minor; the addition of a one- or two-note drone.

v)   Get the groups to name the pieces produced in *J* and iv) and discuss the suitability of these titles.

vi) For keyboard spacings, try using the notes of the triad in harmonic series order — see Activity 17 of *Timbre and Texture*.

Discussion points

–   How does the use of inversion affect the sound of a triad?
–   Are there any spacings so wide that all sense of the triad relationship is lost?
–   Are some spacings of triads (especially minor triads) more expressive than others?

5 Tonic and submediant triads

This activity explores the tonic and submediant triads (I and VI), the notes of which are all contained in the major pentatonic scale.

Preparation

This activity calls for instruments (keyboards and guitars).

Procedure

A   Revise the major pentatonic scale (Activity 4 of *Pitch and Melody*). It is necessary to choose the pitch of this scale with some care: the notes *la*, [ie. lower *la*] *do mi* and *so* must be available to all the voices/instruments being used.

B From this scale get the students to play/sing in sequence the notes *do mi* and *so* (ie. the tonic, mediant and dominant). This forms the tonic major triad covered in Activity 2.

C Repeat *B* as a sustained chord rather than an arpeggio. The students will first have to be divided into three groups where the triad is being sung or played on instruments not capable of producing chords.

D Repeat *B* and *C* for the notes *do mi* and *la* (ie. the tonic, mediant and submediant). This forms the first inversion of the submediant minor triad.

E Discuss the differences in sound between the triads.

F Ask the students to sing/play the root, in the lower octave of the scale, of the submediant triad formed in *D* (ie. *la,*).

G Sing/play the two triads, tonic and submediant, both in close root position, first in arpeggio form, then as sustained chords.

H Get the students to sing/play the Negro spiritual *Who's dat yonder.*

The pitch of this example is for use with the chords G major/E minor only. It should be transposed to the pitch corresponding to the chords used at *G*.

I Divide the class into small groups.

J While one member of each group sings/plays this spiritual, get the others to work out an accompaniment for it at a keyboard or with a guitar, using the two triads.

K Get each group in turn to perform its arrangement.

L Compare and discuss the results.

Variations and extensions

i) Discuss the use of the submediant chord as a substitute for the tonic chord since they share two notes, *do* and *mi*.

ii) In any of the exercises above from *D* onwards, try adding the note *so* to the submediant chord to form a minor 7th chord: *la, do mi so*. Discuss the difference this makes to the harmonisations performed at *K*. The minor 7th chord forms the basis of the activity following (6).

iii) Other tunes that can be harmonised using just I and VI (or VI[7]) include *Morning Mood* from Grieg's music to *Peer Gynt* (see Activity 4 of *Pitch and Melody*), *Shout* (Lulu's famous hit), and further spirituals, such as *Steal Away*.

Further Study

Ensemble Piece No.2 uses only chords I and VI (C major and A minor). The score can be found in the separate *Ensemble Scores* volume and the parts in Unit 5 of the instrumental workbooks. The tonic and submediant triads themselves are introduced in Unit 4 of the workbooks: students are also taught there how to invent simple tunes to go over these triads.

6 One-chord groove

This activity experiments with building up a composition from a single chord.

Preparation

This activity calls for guitars, bass guitar (optional) and keyboards.

Procedure

A   Revise the minor 7th chord . This may be done by going over Activity 5, including variation ii). Alternatively, revise the minor pentatonic scale introduced in Activity 3 of *Pitch and Melody*, and form a chord of the 1st, 2nd, 4th and 5th notes (*la, do mi so*). NB. Use of the E minor pitch facilitates the introduction of guitars later.

B   Form the students into a circle.

C   Build up the minor 7th chord round the circle: the 1st, 5th and 9th students singing E; the 2nd, 6th and 10th, G; the 3rd etc, B; the 4th etc, D, and so on.

D   Whilst this chord is held, get each student in turn to invent a simple bass riff around the root of the chord (E). A drum kit or drum machine accompaniment will help to give the riffs a rhythmic context.

E   Choose the most effective of these riffs.

F   Play this riff on bass guitar or keyboard against the chord. At this stage the chord may be transferred to guitars and/or keyboards as a rhythmic riff in a pattern such as:

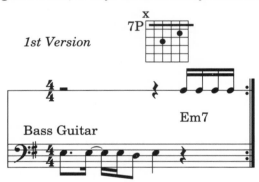

G   Develop this pattern by filling in the rests, as, for instance:

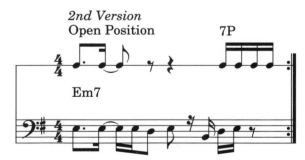

or by experimenting with various added contrasting patterns.

H   Once the rhythm-and-bass pattern of G has the right "feel", get the students in turn to invent melodic riffs around the remaining notes of the chord, G, B and D.

90   *Harmony*

Variations and extensions

i) Add some breaks (eg. bars 5–6 out of every six bars) where students in turn have solo improvisations or where everyone plays the same riff in unison.

ii) Vary the pattern at *G* by transposing it up a tone. Use the two chords to give some sense of progression or structure.

Further study

Limited chord movement, often around a single chord, is a characteristic of some funk and jazz-funk music, for instance that of David Sanborn. Also listen to Ry Cooder's *Down in Hollywood*, from the album *Bop Till You Drop* (MCA MCL 176), Simply Red's *No Direction*, and James Brown's version of *Get up offa that thing* (*The Best of James Brown*, KTEL NE 1376).

Activities 7–12

 AIMS

1 To introduce and consolidate the idea of primary chord progressions.

2 To introduce a standard 12-bar blues harmony.

3 To introduce cadences (perfect/imperfect) and the harmonisation of simple melodies.

4 To explore further the difference between major and minor chords.

5 To explore how melodies can imply harmonies.

7 Tonic and dominant

This activity introduces the dominant chord and shows how this can be used with the tonic chord to make a simple harmonisation.

Procedure

A Form the students into a circle.

B Revise the major scale as introduced in Activity 7 of *Pitch and Melody*. It will be necessary to choose a key in which the voices/instruments being used can cover a range from the lower dominant (*so,*) to the higher tonic (*do'*); the following account

takes the key of C as its example: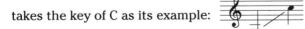

C   Get the students to sing only the first, third, fifth and eighth notes of the scale —

D   Go round the circle repeating the notes of *B*, each student taking one note and holding it as long as possible, as follows:

E   Repeat as a single simultaneous chord, each student repeating the note sung under *D*.
F   Repeat the scale, this time extending it to the lower dominant.
G   As at *B*, get the students to sing pitches 5, 7, 2 and 5 (*so, ti, re so*) of this extended scale —

H   Repeat *D* and *E* using this new chord.
I   Split the circle into two groups.
J   Get the first group to sing the tonic chord: that is each student should sing the note allocated under *D/E*. Make any necessary amendments.
K   In the same way, get the second group to sing the dominant chord: that is each student should sing the note allocated under *G/H*.
L   Point out that between them, these two chords cover all the notes of the scale except *fa* and *la* (in C major, the notes F and A).
M   Sing/play to the students a tune capable of harmonisation by just tonic and dominant chords, such as the theme from the Largo of Dvořák's *New World* Symphony:

Largo

N   Repeat the tune, getting the two groups to add their chord where it seems appropriate. It is preferable for the students to sing the chords, but if this is going to prove difficult, instruments could be used.

Variations and extensions

i) Revoice the two chords to make the transition between them smooth, as for instance:

Repeat *N* with each student participating in both chords.

ii) Introduce the concept of a cadence, a sequence of chords to close a musical phrase. Identify the imperfect cadence (I–V) such as is used in the first two bars of the Dvořák example above, making the tune and harmony seem unfinished. Contrast with the perfect cadence (V–I) which ends the same example, suggesting resolution and completion, in fact "home-coming".

iii) Repeat some of the material using guitars. If both E strings are retuned to D, the B string to A and the G string to F sharp, the open strings give a tonic chord in D major: the dominant chord can then be obtained by barring all the strings at the fifth fret.

iv) The following activity (8) is a simple extension to the present one, adding the third primary chord, the subdominant.

Discussion points

– Do all notes of a melody need to be harmonised?

Further study

The first movement second subject of Beethoven's Fifth Piano Concerto (the *Emperor*) provides a curious example of a melody in which every note is harmonised with either tonic or dominant chord, almost throughout in root position:

8 Tonic, dominant and subdominant

This activity is an extension of the previous one, introducing the third primary chord, the subdominant.

Procedure

A   Revise the two chords (tonic and dominant) introduced in Activity 7 in the same four-note format, but this time sing the dominant chord in the position above the tonic rather than below. It will be necessary to choose a key in which the class taken as a whole has access to a range corresponding to:

B   Introduce the subdominant chord in the position a tone below the dominant as used in *A*. This should be done by forming the basic triad from the fourth, sixth and eighth notes of the scale chosen under *A* and doubling the root at the upper octave to match the two chords already learnt.

C   Introduce the Roman numbers customarily used to identify these chords in discussions of harmony: I = tonic, IV = subdominant, V = dominant.

D   Get the class to make a diagram showing notes making up the three triads. The notes of the major scale should be set vertically up the left hand side of the diagram in either arabic numerals or solfa notation: in either case the notation should reach to the higher supertonic. You might mark the root of each triad with a capital R and the other notes with a star, along the lines shown opposite.

E   Point out that each of the seven different notes making up the scale is covered by at least one chord. It would therefore be possible to harmonise a tune that did not deviate from the scale using just these three chords.

Pitches ↓			
2'			*
1'		*	
7			*
6		*	
5	*		R
4		R	
3	*		
2			
1	R		
Chords →	I	IV	V

F   Divide the class into three chord-groups.

G   Sub-divide the chord I-group into four, and allot the root, third, fifth and octave of the tonic chord amongst them.

H   Get the I group to sing its chord, and correct as necessary.

I   Repeat *G* and *H* for the chord IV-group and chord V-group.

J   Sing/play to the class a tune/tunes requiring slow-moving harmonisation by chords I, IV and V. Examples include: *Oh, when the saints* and *Waltzing Matilda*, the main first movement theme from Mozart's *Eine kleine Nachtmusik*, the slow movement theme from Haydn's Symphony No.94 (the *Surprise*) and many major-key folk-songs and folk-influenced pop songs (eg. early Dylan). The chosen tune(s) may also be performed by a student.

K   Repeat the tune getting the various groups to add their chord where they think appropriate.

L   Assist the process of trial and error to arrive at a satisfactory harmonisation.

M   Perform the tune together with this harmonisation.

N   Present the class with a tune written out in arabic-number or solfa notation (whichever was used under D), a tune such as the traditional South African song *Kum ba yah*:

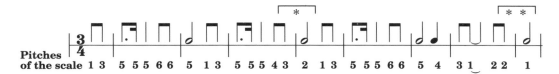

Pitches
of the scale   1 3   5 5 5 6 6   5   1 3   5 5 5 4 3   2   1 3   5 5 5 6 6   5   4   3 1   2 2   1

O   Show how in this way the tune implies its own harmonisation: note 3 (*mi*) belongs to chord I; 4 and 6 (*fa* and *la*) to IV; and 2 and 7 (*re* and *ti*) to V. Note 1 (*do*) belongs to both I and IV; similarly, 5 (*so*) belongs to both I and V. Which is used depends on context and/or personal taste. In the example above, for instance, the first few notes contain both 1 and 5 (*do* and *so*), but the presence of 3 (*mi*) between them implies that all three notes will be harmonised by I.

P   Get the students to mark the chords required by each note, including all the possibilities for 1 and 5 (*do* and *so*).

Q   Play/sing the tune through with the indicated harmonies. Decide between the various possibilities by trial and error.

Variations and extensions

i)   Point out the use of perfect and imperfect cadences. *Kum ba yah* above has an imperfect cadence (*) halfway through and a perfect cadence (**) at the end.

ii) Take any of the chord patterns worked out above, remove the tune it was meant for, and get the students (individually or in small groups) to devise another tune to take its place. Note that the number technique used under *O* above can be used in reverse, with the chords suggesting possible melody notes.

iii) Extend the use of V to include the seventh chord (otherwise covered only in Activity 9 following). The dominant seventh chord is actually implied in the Haydn and Mozart examples suggested in J above.

NB. You might find it useful to keep the chord-graphs made in *D* above for further use in Activity 14.

9 12-Bar blues harmony

This activity introduces the dominant seventh chord and explores how the primary chords (I, IV and V) are used as the harmonic basis of the standard 12-bar blues.

Preparation

This activity calls for instruments.

Procedure

A   Revise the three chords explored in Activity 8.

B   Introduce the dominant 7th chord (V^7), or revise if covered in variation iii) of Activity 8. Explain V^7 as a normal four-note dominant chord in which the doubled root (5' or *so*', depending on notation) has dropped down a tone to 4'/*fa*', as follows:

 . Pass these two forms of the chord round a circle after the manner of *C — E* of Activity 7.

C   Get the students to sing/play the following chord progression:

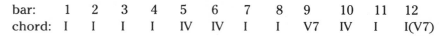

I   IV   V   I

(Adjust key to suit available voices/instruments.)

D   Repeat, substituting V⁷ for V as follows:

I   IV   V⁷   I

E   Discuss the difference in effect between the two progressions. The students should feel the greater sense of direction given to the harmony by the seventh in the dominant chord. Explain how this effect is achieved: the strong pull of the semitones B–C and F–E, and, more importantly, the great need for resolution set up by the discordant combination G/F in the V⁷ chord.

F   Divide the students into small groups of up to six players.

G   Get the groups to play through the standard chord progression of the 12-bar blues:

bar:	1	2	3	4	5	6	7	8	9	10	11	12
chord:	I	I	I	I	IV	IV	I	I	V7	IV	I	I(V7)

H   Add a repeated-figure bass line emphasising the tonic and dominant notes of each chord, such as:

Chord I   Chord IV   Chord V

Adjust the key to match that established in *C* above. Point out that the notes marked (*) do not actually belong to the chords in question, but are merely *melodic decorations* of the bass line.

I   Once the chord progression and bass line are secure, get students to improvise melodic riffs using the pentatonic minor scale (introduced in Activity 9 of *Pitch and Melody*), but based on the same tonic note as that used in *G* above — ie. C minor pentatonic with C major chords.

Variations and extensions

i) In D above explain how the fifth of the chord has been omitted to allow the best part movement between the chords. In four-part harmony, triads must obviously have one note doubled to provide the four parts; but when a fourth note is added to the basic chord, such as the 7th in V⁷, it is still common for a note to be doubled, which means that another note (often the fifth) has to be omitted.

ii) In the melodic riffs of *I*, experiment with the "blue" note, ie. flattening the third of each chord (in the melody only). Everything necessary for such chromatic inflection is dealt with in Activities 21 and 22 of *Pitch and Melody*.

iii) Activity 15 forms a follow-up to the present activity: in it flattened 7ths are added to all three chords, and the melodic riffs are improvised in question-and-answer format.

Further study

Ensemble Piece No.6 is based on a 12-bar blues in C major (with provision for improvisation using C minor pentatonic). The score can be found in the separate *Ensemble Scores* volume and the parts in Unit 13 of the instrumental workbooks.

There is no lack of recorded and printed music based on this pattern of 12-bar blues, in both blues music and early rock n' roll. For more structured listening on the blues, there is P. Oliver's compilation *The Story of the Blues* (CBS 22135).

10 Common chord progressions 1 (I-VI-IV-V)

This activity introduces the common chord progression I–VI–IV–V, used in many popular songs.

Preparation

This activity calls for:
- keyboards
- commercial recordings (suggestions under *F*)

Procedure

A Revise the chord progression from *C* of the previous activity (9), getting the students to sing it in four parts:

I.   IV   V   I

p

B Adapt this by removing the last chord and placing a new intermediate chord between the first and second in the example, getting the students to sing this as well:

I   VI   IV   V

C Identify the new chord as VI, so called because its root is the sixth note of the scale in question (here C major). It has already featured in Activity 5.

D Get the students to work out more idiomatic keyboard figurations for this chord sequence, in a $\frac{4}{4}$ rhythm. These could be based on the fact that the triads (and hence finger patterns) drop down two notes, then another, and finally rise a note:

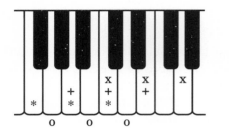

x = Chord I
+ = Chord VI
* = Chord IV
o = Chord V

E Get each student in turn to play through the chosen pattern, allowing one bar to each chord.

F Play recordings of songs based on this pattern, such as: *Wonderful World* and *Only Sixteen* (Sam Cooke), *Dream* (Everly Brothers), *Only You* (Yazoo), *This Boy* (Lennon and McCartney) and *Stand by Me* (Ben E. King). Get the students to identify with the chord change. It is a good idea to use the lyrics and underline the words on which the chord changes occur.

G Repeat some or all of these recordings, getting the students to work out the rhythmic patterns used.

Variations and extensions

i) Get the students to work out their own rhythmic patterns for these chords.

ii) Try building several of these patterns up into a layered harmonic/rhythmic texture.

iii) Explain that the four-chord pattern as it stands is incomplete: the V chord at the end desperately wants to be followed by I. This happens, of course, every time the whole pattern is repeated (I–VI–IV–V–I–VI–IV–V–I etc), but at the end of the piece a final tonic chord has to be added.

11 Um-cha-cha accompaniment

This activity explores the I–IV–V⁷–I chord sequence in the accompaniment pattern common to most waltzes.

Preparation

This activity calls for instruments.

Procedure

A Distribute the instruments amongst the students.

B   Get the students to play through the following chord sequence:

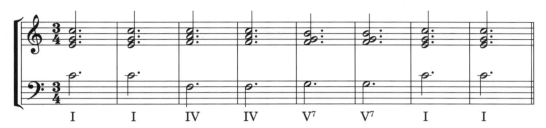

I   I   IV   IV   V⁷   V⁷   I   I

Transpose *ad lib.* to suit the instruments being used. (If any revision is needed to cover this progression, see Activity 9.)

C   Repeat this progression using the following figuration: the bass note (root) of each chord in dotted minims, lasting the whole of each bar, and the remaining three notes as crotchet chords on the second and third beats of each bar, as follows:

etc.

D   Vary the bass pattern by alternating the root and the lower fifth, as follows. Use chord I only at this stage:

E   Repeat for the other chords in turn.
F   Apply this pattern to the chord sequence from *B*.
G   Using the "um-cha-cha" figure, get the students to work out a harmonic accompaniment to a waltz tune, such as the main theme from Johann Strauss's *The Blue Danube*.

Variations and extensions

i) Transpose the accompaniment pattern to various other keys.
ii) Vary the "cha-cha" chords by allowing students to change the octave in which they play their note at will.
iii) Experiment with moving the "cha-cha" chords as well as the bass:

iv) Try adding a quaver note between the two "cha-cha" chords, in the pattern:

Get the students to experiment with different notes for this quaver and see which they find most appropriate and/or interesting.

v) Get the students to repeat their accompaniment from *G* and devise melodies of their own for it. The melodies should be suggested by the notes in the supporting harmony.

vi) Compare this accompaniment pattern with that used in marches and folksongs. The principle is the same, except that marches and most folk music are in $\frac{4}{4}$ or $\frac{2}{4}$ time — "um-pa um-pa", rather than "um-cha-cha". The bass also frequently alternates the root and lower fifth, though every two beats rather than every three: this is a feature, for instance, of Scott Joplin rags and Sousa marches. You can often hear this same bass movement in Country and Western music.

Discussion points

– What is the effect of using the fifth in the bass?
– Were there any bars in *The Blue Danube* where the "um-cha-cha" pattern did not sound quite right? Why should that be?

Further study

There is no lack of recorded examples of waltz music with "um-cha-cha" accompaniments. As a curiosity, Chopin's Waltz in A flat, Op.42, has this pattern clearly in the left hand, but the tune above is a straight two-in-the-bar.

12 Neighbour-note chord changes

This activity looks at chords moving in parallel between neighbouring notes. In particular, it explores the major-to-minor, neighbour-chord alternations found in many varieties of reggae music.

Procedure

A   Revise the natural minor scale introduced in Activity 10 of *Pitch and Melody*:

B   Working around a circle, build up a four-note chord based on the tonic of this scale  , by the method familiar from Activities 7–9.

C   Repeat for the chord on the leading note  , pointing

out that the leading note's being flattened will result in a *major* chord here.

D   In a slow $\frac{4}{4}$, get the class to alternate one bar of crotchet chords of I with one of bVII, as follows:

E   Repeat with the chords moved on to quaver offbeats:

F   Repeat *E* with the addition of bass riffs derived from the chords, such as:

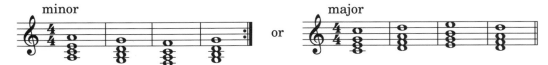

G   When this is stable, get the students to invent melodic riffs which a) use the natural minor scale and b) fit the harmonic pattern.

Variations and extensions

i)   Repeat the exercises using the major scale and alternating chords I and II. The major and minor chords will be the opposite way round to the above.

ii)   Extend the parallel chord movement one neighbour note further, that is:

minor   major

 or

Further study

Many forms of reggae have this kind of chord progression at their heart. The verse of Dylan's *All along the Watchtower* is based on the progression I–bVII–bVI–bVII in A minor. Lionel Ritchie's *All Night Long* is in a major key, but has a chorus based on the chords I and bVII and a verse using the progression I–bVII–II–I. The verse of Lennon and McCartney's *Here, there and everywhere* (from the album *Revolver*) has the chord progression I–II⁷–III⁷–IV. Similar chord sequences lie behind some of Debussy's piano music (for instance *Hommage à Rameau* from the first book of piano *Images*) and the three *Gymnopédie*s by Erik Satie.

   Ensemble Piece No.9 makes prominent use of the progression III–II–I. The score can be found in the separate *Ensemble Scores* volume and the parts in Unit 19 of the instrumental workbooks.

Activities 13–18

1 To explore additional common chord progressions, including secondary chords.
2 To introduce major seventh chords.
3 To develop an understanding of chord inversions.
4 To explore pedal notes.
5 To develop further an understanding of cadences, introducing both plagal and interrupted.

13 Common chord progressions 2 (I-VI-II-V)

This activity introduces the supertonic chord, built on the second note of a major scale; it shows how this is used as an approach chord at cadences and, with a sharpened third, in modulating to the dominant.

Preparation

This activity calls for:
– instruments (optional)
– commercial recordings (suggestions under *M*)

Procedure

A   Get the class to sing a major scale.
B   Form a four-note chord from notes 2 4 6 and 2' of this scale, by the method familiar from Activities 7 and 8. [This chord was introduced, in passing, in variation i) of Activity 12, and it may only be necessary to revise this to re-introduce the chord.]
C   Identify the chord as II, so-called because its root is the second note of the major scale.
D   Divide the students into four groups, one to take each note in the four-part harmony to follow. Where the harmony is to be sung, division into groups should take account of voice ranges.
E   Get the students to play/sing through the following chord progression.

F   By the time this is perfected, each student will perceive the group's contribution melodically, as a sequence of three notes. It is important at this stage to impress on the students the vertical, ie. harmonic, significance of each note.

G   Repeat *E* in a different rhythm.

H   Repeat *E* in a different key.

I   Continue experimenting with different keys and rhythms/metres.

J   Get the students to sing/play the chord sequence from *B* of Activity 10.

K   Repeat this, substituting II for IV as the third chord:

L   Repeat this new progression in a variety of keys and rhythms/metres.

M   Play recordings of songs which use this progression, such as Rodgers and Hart's *Blue Moon*, Neil Sedaka's *Breaking up is hard to do* and Stevie Wonder's *Lately*, where it is used at the beginning of the verse.

Variations and extensions

i)   Get the students to invent simple rhythmic figurations for this chord sequence.

ii) Try inventing short tunes which fit the chord sequence, using the notes of the chords themselves as a guide.

iii) Get the students to plot chord II on their chord charts (see Activity 8). This will underline that chord II is a minor one, with the major 3rd lying at the top.

Discussion points

– Why is it so easy to replace IV with II at *K*?

– Why is the progression II–V–I so strong?

14 Major seventh chords

This activity introduces and explores major seventh chords.

Procedure

A   Return to the chord-graphs students made of triads I, IV and V at D in Activity 8.

B   Complete or re-do these graphs showing triads rooted on every note of the major scale.

C   Get the class to sing up and down each triad in turn.

D   Add another note to the top of each triad, a third higher than the top note itself, ie. a seventh higher than the root. The result should look like this:

Pitches ↓

Pitches	I	II	III	IV	V	VI	VII
6'							*
5'						*	
4'					*		○
3'				*		○	
2'			*		○		+
1'		*		○		+	
7	*		○		+		r
6		○		+		r	
5	○		+		r		
4		+		r			
3	+		r				
2		r					
1	r						
Chords →	I	II	III	IV	V	VI	VII

r = root of the chord
+ = 3rd of the chord
○ = 5th of the chord
* = 7th of the chord

E   Get the class to sing up and down each of these new chords in turn. Guard carefully against the natural instinct to sing the octave rather than the seventh at the top.

F   Distribute instruments as appropriate/available.

G   Repeat the chords of *E*, played on instruments. It may be necessary to divide the students into four groups, one each taking the root, third, fifth and seventh of the chords.

H   Discuss the effect of these seventh chords, particularly the major seventh chords I and IV.

I   Get the students to play these two chords in alternation:

J   Play recordings of music featuring chords of this type. Two good examples are Erik Satie's popular *Gymnopédie No.1* and Bacharach and David's song *This guy's in love with you*. Arrangements of the Satie work can be found in Unit 16 of the Guitar, Bass Guitar and Keyboard Workbooks which complement this volume.

Variations and extensions

i)   Get the students to sing/play through the following progression showing the variety of seventh chords that can be based on any given root:

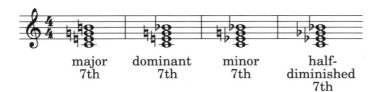

major   dominant   minor   half-
7th   7th   7th   diminished
                                                   7th

ii) Activity 15 forms an extension to the present one, applying sevenths to the chord sequence of the 12-bar blues introduced in Activity 9.

Discussion points

- What kind of effects does the major seventh create?
- Are any seventh chords possible other than those of variation i)?

15 12-Bar blues harmony: Variation 1

This activity is a follow-up to Activities 9 and 14, adding the sevenths of the latter to the basic 12-bar blues chord sequence of the former.

Preparation

Activity 15 may be either sung or played. It is quite a good idea to begin with singing and go on to instruments: in which case, sing steps *A–F*, repeat *F* on instruments, and stay with the instruments to the end.

Procedure

A   Revise Activity 14.
B   Isolate chords I⁷, IV⁷ and V⁷.
C   Change the I and IV chords so they become the flattened seventh chords I♭⁷ and IV♭⁷, to match V⁷.
D   Revise the chord progression of the 12-bar blues, introduced in Activity 9.
E   Repeat *D* substituting I⁷, IV⁷ and V⁷ for I, IV and V.
F   Add the following bass line to *E*:

Transpose as necessary.
G   When this is secure, revise (if necessary) question-and-answer melodic construction and the pentatonic minor scale (Activities 5 and 9 of *Pitch and Melody*).

H   Get the students in pairs to improvise melodies over the 12-bar blues chord-and-bass accompaniment pattern of *F*. The melodies should use the notes of the minor pentatonic scale, and the student pairs should alternate two-bar phrases, the first student (b. 1/2, 5/6 and 9/10) putting melodic questions and the second student (b. 3/4, 7/8 and 11/12) providing melodic answers.

Variations and extensions

i)   A further extension can be found in Activity 21, where the familiar chord sequence is treated to sixth and ninth chords. Further work is done on the blues in Activities 9 and 10 of *Structure and Form*.

Discussion points

–   Do the flattened seventh chords undermine the sense of key?

16 First-inversion substitutes

This activity explores the use of the first inversion to replace root-position chords in the harmonisation of simple melodies.

Procedure

A   Play the students the following chord progression:

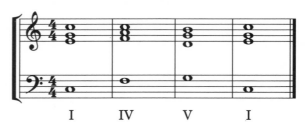

    I   IV   V   I

B   Get the students to try identifying the chords.
C   Repeat the chord sequence, adding first inversion chords before each chord change:

    I   Ib   IV   IVb   V   Vb   I

D   Ask the students to describe the changes made.

E Discuss the answers, then explain and demonstrate how a first inversion is related to a root-position chord.

F Explain that in the system which describes chords by the use of Roman numerals (I, IV, V etc), these numerals are used only for root-position chords: first inversions are indicated by the use of a lower-case b after the numeral (Ib, IVb, Vb etc.).

G Repeat the chord sequence of *C*, identifying each chord by its symbol: I, Ib, IV etc.

H Play the bass lines only of *A* and *C*, and note how much smoother *C* is. This is one of the main reasons for using first inversions.

I Give the students some simple melodies, such as the following, to harmonise using root position chords.

NB. Any melodies given should be of a type and length appropriate to the improvisation (pitch) section of the unprepared performance part of the GCSE examination. The above examples take this into consideration.

J Get the students to reharmonise the melodies using first-inversion chords where these will give a smoother bass line.

Variations and extensions

i) Introduce the common cadential formula IIb–V⁷–I, linking this to the work on the supertonic chord in Activity 13. See how many of the melodies in I above can make use of this formula.

ii) Analyse with the class a well-known piece in four-part harmony, preferably one rich in first inversions. *God save the Queen* is a good example. If any second inversions occur, explain them in passing, introducing the notation Ic, Vc etc. Any instances of the expansion of the formula mentioned in var. i) to IIb–Ic–V⁷–I should also be noted and discussed.

iii) Get the students to invent a melody to fit the chord sequence of *C* above.

17 Pedal notes

This activity introduces pedal notes and explores their effect.

Preparation

This activity calls for instruments, some of which must be capable of taking a bass line.

Procedure

A   Divide the students into two disproportionate groups, the larger to take the chords, the smaller for a bass line.

B   Select a key and invent a progression of around 6–8 chords, such as the following: I–IV–V⁷–I–VI⁷–IV–I.

C   Get the chord group to play this sequence. In cases of difficulty, each line of the harmony could be rote-learnt as a melody; or the group subdivided, with one sub-group playing chord I, another chord IV etc.

D   Repeat *C* with the bass group sustaining a tonic pedal in the bass. Methods for sustaining the note will vary with the instrument(s) used, but naturally-occurring staggered repeats should ensure continuity.

E   Compare and discuss the two versions, if necessary repeating them. Note above all that the tonic pedal exerts a strong pull towards the tonic chord. Note also that chords containing the tonic note (I, IV and VI) sound more "at home" over a tonic pedal than, say, the dominant, where notes 2 and 7 of the scale clash with note 1:

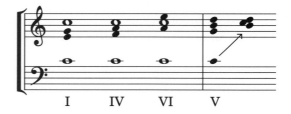

I   IV   VI   V

Explain that chord IV put over a tonic pedal results in the second inversion chord IVc. Ask if the progression I–IV over a tonic pedal sounds familiar: it is commonly used in popular songs.

F   Divide the students into small groups and get them to experiment with chord progressions over tonic pedals.

G   If the suggested Largo from Dvořák's *New World Symphony* was used as a melody to harmonise with just chords I and V in *M* of Activity 7 above, remind the students of this.

H   Play the Largo in its proper harmonisation, using pedal notes:

Largo

Cor anglais

I   V⁷   I   (III♯³ aug)   II♭⁷   V⁷   I

Pedals: tonic ——————————————————————————————

IV   (V   IV)   IV   (V   IV)

tonic ——————————————————— dom. ———————————

subdom. ———————————————————— tonic ——————————

I   Vb   VI   Ic   IV   I   II♭⁷   I   II♭⁷   I

dom.——————————

dom.———————————————

——————————

I   Point out the various features of the harmony: the pedals (including sub-dominant and dominant examples), the augmented chord used in passing in b.3, and the IIb–V–I formula in b.4.

J   Play a recording of the Largo's opening played by an orchestra in the proper key (D flat major).

Variations and extensions

i)   Play the chord progression of *B* over a tonic pedal, then over a dominant pedal. Repeat the dominant pedal version, but ending on a root-position tonic chord. Discuss the differences in effect. Refer back to the discussion of *E* above. Note that with a dominant pedal, V becomes a root-position chord, and that III is now concordant while IV and VI are discordant. Moreover, I becomes the second-inversion chord Ic. This new chord can be used to expand the familiar IIb–V7–I formula to IIb–Ic–V⁷–I.

ii) Experiment to find a chord sequence better suited to a dominant pedal, such as: I-IV–V⁷–II–I–V⁷–I.

iii) Explain the purpose and use of pedals, playing examples wherever possible.

The *dominant pedal*, as will have been felt from i), expects to lead to a root-position chord of I. The longer that "resolution" is delayed, the greater the sense of anticipation and tension. So powerful is this tension, that composers have used dominant pedals to introduce structurally important appearances of the tonic key. Most commonly, it re-introduces the tonic key at the recapitulation of a sonata-form movement (eg. the first movement of Beethoven's *Eroica* Symphony, or the finale of the Seventh) or leads to a final, culminating climax (Brahms' *Handel Variations*, Op.24, the finale of Rakhmaninov's Third Piano Concerto [fig.69ff.] or the scherzo of his Second Symphony [*Con moto* after figs.29/41]).

The *tonic pedal*, on the other hand, tends to feel more static, and is often used at the end of pieces that need the effect of a lot of tonic chord, without the monotony of repeating that chord constantly (eg. end of Bach's Second *Brandenburg* Concerto or of Shostakovich's Fourth Symphony — in the last named the pedal lasts several minutes). A tonic pedal is sometimes used under a theme (opening of the finale of Haydn's Symphony No.104, or of the first movement of Bach's Sixth *Brandenburg* Concerto), and is often used for special effect, such as monumental (opening to Strauss' *Also sprach Zarathustra*) or menacing (opening to Holst's suite *The Planets*). Some examples in popular music are Billy Joel's *Just the way you are* (tonic pedal introduction), Survivor's *Eye of the tiger* (pounding tonic pedal below neighbour-note chord movement) and Genesis' *Turn it on again* (two pedal notes, one after the other, a semitone apart).

iv) Discuss the suitability of various instruments to sustain a pedal line. The instrument which has the least problem holding notes indefinitely is the organ, for which the device was probably invented — hence the name. The pedal board of the organ is ideally suited to "pedal" notes and organ literature abounds with them.

v) Mention the "inverted pedal", the technical name for a pedal note which is not in the bass. A good example is the repeated treble B♭ throughout *Le gibet* from Ravel's *Gaspard de la nuit*.

18 Plagal and interrupted cadences

This activity introduces plagal and interrupted cadences.

Preparation

This activity calls for commercial recordings of pieces containing examples of plagal and interrupted cadences.

Plagal cadences can be found in Lennon and McCartney's *Yesterday* and Curtis Mayfield's *People get ready* (which uses the progression in *B* below); or, in classical music, at the end of the *Hallelujah* chorus from Handel's *Messiah* and of Mendelssohn's overture to *A midsummer night's dream*.

Interrupted cadences can be found in Police's *Ev'ry breath you take* (which uses the progression in *D* below, decorated with ninth chords) and in Schumann's song *Was machte dich so krank?* (Op.35 No.11), where the vocal part ends on chord VI while the piano postlude resolves this with a perfect cadence.

Very clear examples of matching phrases with interrupted then plagal cadences can be found in the earliest music of Mozart, the B♭ Allegro (K.3) and the F major Minuet (K.2), which may well be familiar to any budding pianists among the students.

Procedure

A   Remind the students of the concept of cadence, revising from Activity 7 as necessary.

B   Get the students to sing/play through the following chord progression in a suitable major key: I–VI–IV–I.

C   Explain that an ending such as this, finishing on the progression IV–I is called a "Plagal cadence". Those who attend very traditional protestant churches may recognise the formula as the chords used for the "Amen" at the end of hymns.

D   Get the students to sing/play through the following chord progression in a suitable major key: I–VI–IV–V–VI.

E   Explain that an ending such as this, finishing on the progression V–VI is called an "Interrupted cadence".

F   Repeat D twice more, getting the students to substitute I for the final VI the last time through.

G   Explain that up until the final chord, the progression really expects to end in a perfect cadence V–I. The substitution of the related (they share two notes), but unexpected, chord VI for the expected I constitutes the surprise "interruption". Pieces rarely end on anything but the tonic, however, so where an interrupted cadence is used, the music leading up to it is generally repeated immediately afterwards, finishing with a perfect cadence.

H   Play recordings of pieces containing examples of plagal and interrupted cadences.

I   Get the students (individually or in small groups) to harmonise the traditional Scottish melody *Ye banks and braes*, drawing attention to its implied plagal cadence:

J   Perform the results.

K   Compare the results with the following harmonisation, which uses tonic pedals:

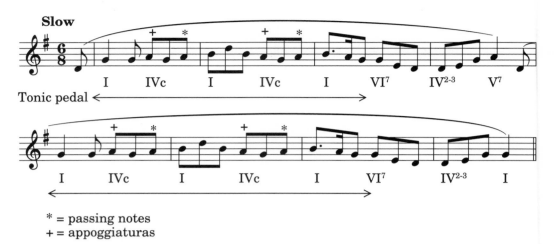

Slow

I   IVc   I   IVc   I   VI^7 IV$^{2-3}$ V^7

Tonic pedal ←———————————————→

I   IVc   I   IVc   I   VI^7 IV$^{2-3}$ I

←———————————————→

* = passing notes
+ = appoggiaturas

Variations and extensions

i) Explain the use of passing notes and appoggiaturas in the *K* harmonisation.

ii) Try using plagal and interrupted cadences at the end of progressions in minor keys. In a plagal cadence, both chords will now be minor chords, whereas both chords of an interrupted cadence will be major. Further work on minor-key harmony is done in the remaining activities of this chapter.

iii) Experiment with chords other than VI at the end of a phrase to produce a surprise effect. What other chords could follow V to create this "interrupted" feel?

Activities 19—24

AIMS

1 To introduce minor harmony*.
2 To explore chords with added notes — 6ths and 9ths.
3 To introduce diminished-seventh and augmented chords.
4 To explore suspensions.
5 To explore extended cadential progressions.

* The discussion of minor harmony is complicated by the presence of so many different forms of minor scale — natural (ie Aeolian), melodic, harmonic, not to mention various modal inflections. The approach in this book is to deal first (Activity 19) with minor harmony derived exclusively from the natural minor scale (the form that has no deviations from the proper key signature), and then (Activity 20) to show how the harmony is altered to give major forms of chord V etc.

19 Minor harmony 1

This activity introduces harmony built up from the notes of the natural minor scale.

Procedure

A   Revise the natural minor scale introduced in Activity 10 of *Pitch and Melody*.

B   Remind the students of the diagrams of chords I, IV and V they produced in Activity 8 (of the present chapter).

C   Get the students to produce a corresponding diagram for triads built on *all* the notes of the natural minor scale, along the lines of:

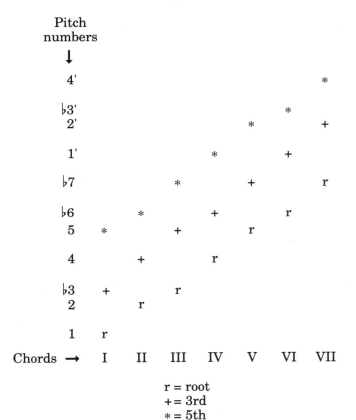

Pitch
numbers

	I	II	III	IV	V	VI	VII
4'							*
♭3'						*	
2'					*		+
1'				*		+	
♭7			*		+		r
♭6		*		+		r	
5	*		+		r		
4		+		r			
♭3	+		r				
2		r					
1	r						
Chords →	I	II	III	IV	V	VI	VII

r = root
+ = 3rd
* = 5th

D   Get the students to play/sing through the triads in turn, if necessary forming three groups to supply the root, third and fifth of each chord.

E   Repeat *D*, asking the students to identify each triad in turn as major (III, VI and VII), minor (I, IV and V) or diminished (II).

F   Give the students (individually or in small groups) a melody to harmonise, using chords I, IV and V only. The melody should confine itself to the natural minor scale, a good example being *The wraggle-taggle gipsies, O*:

G   Perform the results in turn and discuss.

Variations and extensions

i)   Consider which chords could act as substitutes for IV and V. Each shares two notes with two other chords — IV with II and VI, V with III and VII:

ii) Experiment with these substitute chords in the harmonisation(s) of *G*.

iii) The following activity (20) is itself an extension to the present one, introducing the changes necessary to cope with the harmonic and melodic minor scales.

20 Minor harmony 2

This activity forms a follow-up to the previous one, expanding the harmony learned there to cope with the harmonic and melodic forms of the minor scale.

Procedure

A   Revise Activity 19 as necessary.

B   As under *F* there, get the students (individually or in small groups) to harmonise, using only chords I, IV and V, the traditional melody *The Bellman's Song*:

C   Collate and discuss the results, paying particular attention to the solutions the students found for harmonising the note G sharp. The most natural course here is to use the major form of chord V. Show how the melody outlines the harmonic minor scale (Activity 19 of *Pitch and Melody*), which is the same as the natural minor scale, but with a raised seventh. Note that this raised seventh will also affect the chords that can be used as substitutes for V, making III an augmented and VII a diminished triad.

D   Get the students to adapt the chord diagrams they produced under *C* of the last activity to incorporate the raised seventh used by the harmonic minor scale.

E Show the students the parallel changes that have to be made when harmonising melodies using the melodic minor scale (Activity 13 of *Pitch and Melody*). Both the sixth and seventh notes of the scale are likely to be raised. The raising of the seventh has already been dealt with: the raising of the sixth note of the scale turns IV into a *major* triad, changing the substitutes II and VI into minor and diminished triads respectively.

It is important to remember, though, that the melodic minor scale contains both raised and unraised sixths and sevenths, and so either form of the appropriate chords may be required. The main theme from the slow movement of Beethoven's Symphony No.7, used in Activity 20 of *Timbre and Texture*, might be a useful one to discuss here.

F Repeat *B* and *C* for a melody using the melodic minor scale.

Variations and extensions

i) Repeat the harmonisations of *B* and *F*, experimenting with the substitutes for IV and V.

ii) Give the students this melody to harmonise:

Traditional carol: *The Saviour's Work*

iii) Get the students to invent melodies using the harmonic and/or melodic minor scales and then to harmonise them.

iv) Introduce the idea of the *tierce de Picardie*, the use of a major tonic chord at the end of what is an otherwise normal piece in the minor. Play through some of the student harmonisations twice, both with and without a *tierce de Picardie* and discuss the difference.

v) Further work on augmented and diminished chords occurs in Activity 22.

21 12-Bar blues harmony: Variation 2

This activity explores the addition to a basic triad of notes other than the seventh, principally the sixth and ninth, applying the resulting chords to the 12-bar blues formula established in Activities 9 and 15 of this chapter.

Procedure

A   Working in a circle, get the students to sing a major triad, using the methods from Activity 3: .

B   Repeat adding the note a tone above the top note of the triad, ie the sixth of the scale: .

C   Carry on building round the circle until the sixth chord is secure.

D   Repeat *A* for the dominant triad: .

E   Repeat, adding the seventh: .

F   Repeat, adding the note a major third above this new top note: .

G   Carry on building round the circle until the ninth chord is secure and sustained.

H   Get the students to resolve this dominant ninth chord on to a tonic triad, the parts moving as follows: .

I   Explain that these complex chords are normally shown by small arabic numbers after the roman chord symbols. V^7 has already been met. The chord from *B* is I^6, and that from *F* V^9. Note that the use of V^9 assumes the presence of a minor seventh in the chord.

J   Get the students to play through, with a 12/8 rhythm, the following variation of the 12-bar blues: I^6 IV^9 I^6 I^6 IV^9 IV^9 I^6 I^6 V^9 IV^9 I^9 V^9.

K   When this is secure, add an appropriate bass line and get the students to improvise melodies, as explained in Activity 15.

Variations and extensions

i)   As an alternative or additional way to introduce the dominant ninth chord, super-impose a supertonic triad on top of a dominant triad as follows:

The root of the II triad is the same note as the fifth of the V.

ii) Try using chords I^6 and V^9 in some of the chord progressions from the activities immediately previous.

iii) Get the students (individually or in small groups) to experiment with other chords built on thirds — seventh and ninth chords (and beyond to 11th and 13th chords) on any note of the scale. Write down any especially interesting ones.

iv) Get the students (again individually or in small groups) to explore various position-ings of the chord I^6, always keeping the root in the bass. Write down any particularly successful versions.

v)   Compare the effects of the following spacings of a ninth chord:

Experiment with other spacings.

Discussion points

- As more and more different notes are added to the basic triad, some notes have to be omitted. Which should be left out?
- How would you describe the difference using these chords makes? Is the music clearer, richer, jazzier, sharper?

Further study

Ensemble Piece No.11 adds sixth and ninth chords to the 12-bar blues. The score can be found in the separate *Ensemble Scores* volume and the parts in Unit 23 of the instrumental workbooks which complement this volume.

22 Augumented and diminished chords

This activity introduces the augmented triad and the chord of the diminished seventh, and explores their use as passing chords.

Procedure

A   Build up a major triad around a circle, finally sustaining it. (The method, also used in the previous activity, can be found in Activity 3.)

B   Get the students taking the top note (fifth) of the triad to sing this by themselves.

C   Get them to sing the note a semitone higher.

D   Repeat the triad produced at A, but with the raised fifth.

Step: A   B   C   D

E   Identify this chord as an augmented triad.

F   Continue building up this augmented triad round the circle, until every student has experienced each note and the chord can be produced at will. If undue difficulty is experienced, the students should practise in groups of three, using instruments as necessary.

G   Divide the students into four parts by vocal range.

H   Get the students to sing through the following progression, choosing a key appropriate to the available voices:

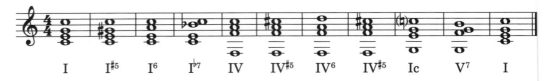

I   I#5   I6   I♭7   IV   IV#5   IV6   IV#5   Ic   V7   I

I   Point out how the raised fifth in the chords marked #5 is part of the *horizontal* movement of that vocal line.

J   Repeat *A*, this time building up a minor triad.

K   Repeat *B–D*, this time flattening the fifth.

L   Add a new note a minor third above the top note:

Step: *J*   *K*   (*K*)   (*K*)   *L*

M   Identify this chord as a diminished seventh. Technically speaking, this last is only a diminished seventh chord if notated thus:  .

N   As at *F*, continue building up this diminished seventh chord round the circle, until every student has experienced each note and the chord can be produced at will. If undue difficulty is experienced, the students should practise in groups of four, using instruments as necessary.

O   As at *G*, divide the students into four parts by vocal range.

P   As at *H*, get the students to sing through the following progressions, choosing a key appropriate to the available voices:

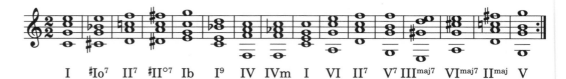

I   #I°7   II7   V7

I   #Io7   II7   #II°7   Ib   I9   IV   IVm   I   VI   II7   V7   IIImaj7   VImaj7   IImaj   V

Q   Point out how the chords marked °7 are used as chromatic passing chords.

Variations and extensions

i)   As an alternative or additional way to introduce these two chords, build them up out of notes taken from the harmonic minor scale as follows:

(In the case of the diminished seventh chord, note the proviso under *M* above.)

ii)   The diminished seventh is a very versatile chord, which can lead in many directions, some of them rather surprising. Get the students (individually or in small groups) to explore and note down the various possibilities.

iii) Play recorded examples of music using these chords, and analyse the progressions.

There are prominent augmented triads in the verse of Masser and Creed's *The greatest love of all* and in choruses from the Gershwin numbers *Of thee I sing* and *Nice work if you can get it*.

Diminished seventh chords are easy to find: in classical music, Bach was especially fond of their flexibility, and many clear examples can be found in the chorale harmon-isations, while in popular music the Beatles made the chord the basis of their song *Wild Honey Pie* from the album *The Beatles* (known as the *White Album*); Kahn and Donaldson's *Makin' Whoopee* is based on the first chord sequence of *P* above, and the second can be used to harmonize the verse of Fats Waller's *Ain't Misbehavin'*.

The Rodgers and Hart number *Bewitched* and Murden's *For once in my life* use both chords.

23 Chord suspensions

This activity introduces chord suspensions and explores their effect.

Preparation

This activity calls for:
- commercial recordings of music by, for example, Corelli, illustrating the type of progression shown under *H* below.
- commercial recordings of well-known tunes making use of suspensions (suggestions under *K* below).

Procedure

A   Divide the students by vocal range into four parts.

B   Get them to sing the following progression, in a suitable key:

C   Repeat, with the top voices only delaying the move to their second note until the *second* beat of the second bar. The remaining three groups move on the first beat as in *B*:

D   Explain that, because of the way the top line seems to be suspended over the change of chord, this device came to be called a "suspension". Note also the way in which this "suspension" of the top line causes the discordant combination of the notes C and D: it is this discord which seems to demand that the top note move down to B. This movement to remove the discord formed by a suspension is known as its "resolution".

E   Repeat the progression of *C* and then the following repositionings, which will give each part an experience of the suspension:

F   Point out that the note on to which the suspension is resolved is best not doubled in the second chord (in *C* above, for instance, there is no B in the second chord until the suspended voice moves from the note C): to do that would undermine the suspension and ruin its effect. The only exception to this rule is in the case of a 9–8 suspension (see b.6 of the following example).

G   Get the students to sing/play the following progression which contains one suspension in each part:

Slow

H   Get the students to sing/play through the following progression. Note the curious way the top two parts seem to tread on each other's toes.

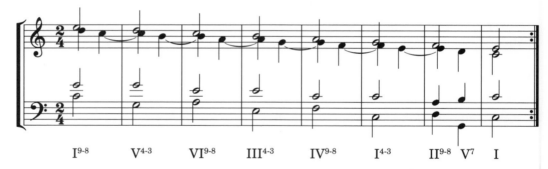

$$\text{I}^{9-8} \qquad \text{V}^{4-3} \qquad \text{VI}^{9-8} \qquad \text{III}^{4-3} \qquad \text{IV}^{9-8} \qquad \text{I}^{4-3} \qquad \text{II}^{9-8} \; \text{V}^7 \quad \text{I}$$

This kind of progression was a particular favourite of 17th-century Italian composers of concerti grossi and instrumental sonatas.

I   Play recorded examples of this sort of music.

J   Point out that suspensions are often used in popular music. Notes here are much less likely to be physically suspended, with one note held through the change of chord. More probably the "suspended" note will be repeated as a decoration.

K   Play recorded examples of this, such as the Who's *Pinball Wizard* and the theme tune to *Neighbours*.

Variations and extensions

i) Get the students in small groups to try out suspensions in a minor key. The progression of *G*, for instance, cannot be transferred as it stands to a minor key. Why not? Where does it need to be adapted or rewritten?

ii) Try using some double suspensions, such as $\begin{smallmatrix}9&8\\4&3\end{smallmatrix}$ or $\begin{smallmatrix}6&5\\4&3\end{smallmatrix}$.

iii) Expand on ii) by introducing the common 18th-century cadential formula:

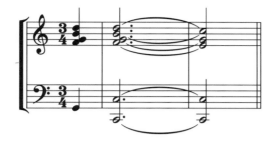

iv) Explore the effect of rising suspensions, such as 7–8 and 2–3. The last named sometimes occurs in popular music, for instance in *24 hours from Tulsa*.

Further study

Ensemble Piece No.8 makes some use of sus 4. The score can be found in the separate *Ensemble Scores* volume and the parts in Unit 17 of the instrumental workbooks.

24 Common chord progressions 3 (cycle of fifths)

This activity links together the seven chords I — VII in a chain sometimes called the 'Cycle of Fifths'.

Procedure

A   Refer back to Activity 13 and revise the chord progression it introduced, choosing a key to suit the instruments/voices available:

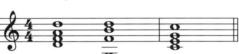

B   Draw attention to the movement between the roots of these chords, a rising fourth or a falling fifth. Explain how these two intervals are really the same.

C   Get the students to extend this progression backwards until they arrive once more at the tonic. The progression they get should include all the notes of the scale and hence each of chords I — VII, thus:

| I | IV | VII | III | VI | II | V | I |

D   Point out that the interval between the roots of IV and VII is a *diminished* fifth.

E   Play to the students the following sequence which uses part of the cycle of fifths as an extension to the chord progression introduced under *I* of Activity 22.

‹- ›
Cycle of fifths

F   Ask the students to identify the popular song from which this is taken. [Masser and Creed's *The greatest love of all*, recorded by various singers, amongst them Whitney Houston]

Variations and extensions

i)   Try the progression of *C* in the minor, using chords derived from the natural minor scale. In this case the diminished fifth will now be between the roots of VI and II.

ii) If you repeat the sequence of *C*, using nothing but perfect fourths and fifths, you will get a chord on every note of the chromatic scale before you reach the starting-point again, as in:

or, using flattened sevenths, the more striking:

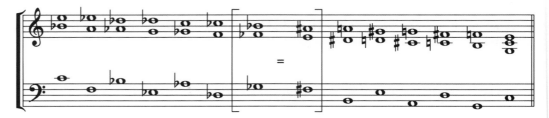

This is called the 'cycle of fifths' and is of fundamental importance to an understanding of key structures and interrelationships. Note how one way from the starting point the chords get flatter and flatter, while the other way they get sharper and sharper, only to meet in the middle where the same chord can be written in both sharps and flats (enharmonics).

Further study

There are many instances of harmony using chains of fifths in this way, for instance the close of the first movement of Beethoven's Piano Sonata in F minor, Op.2 No.1, the chorus to Kern and Hammerstein's *All the things you are* (where the sequence actually starts on chord VI) and in the theme song to the film *Arthur* by Bacharach, Bayer, Sager, Cross and Allen.

Structure and Form

CONTENTS

123

Activities 1–6

1 To contrast the absence of order (ie. chance mechanisms) with planned structures.
2 To explore phrase and sentence structures.
3 To explore simple verse structures.
4 To consider some of the functions of introductions and codas.
5 To explore and create simple two-part rounds.

1 Chance operations

This activity explores what happens when musical ideas are combined by chance mechanisms rather than by deliberate choice. It aims to show the importance of planning a structure and of stylistic consistency.

Preparation

This activity calls for:
– a die
– a tape recorder
while the ancillary sections require:
– recordings already made by the students [see var.i)]
– prepared cards [see var.ii)]

Procedure

A Divide the class into groups of four.
B Within a time limit of 10–15 minutes, each group invents an idea or short (no more than 30 seconds) piece. The ideas can be melodic, harmonic, rhythmic, vocal, instrumental or any combination.
C Each group in turn performs its composition to the whole class.
D Allocate a number order to the groups.
E A die is thrown, and the group whose number comes up plays its composition.
F Repeat E until every group has played its contribution at least once.
G When the groups are familiar with the process, record a "performance" of E and F. You may find it easier to make all the necessary throws of the die in advance, before starting to record.
H Play back the tape and discuss the result. Which ideas work well together, and which do not? Consider the reasons for this.

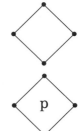

Variations and extensions

i) Get the students to make random recordings of sounds from the local environment. Each recording should contain snippets of sound from various locations, following on without gaps or preconceived order. Discuss the results. Do any of the recordings unintentionally contain order? Do the recorded snippets fit with each other?

ii) As an alternative to *B*, give the groups cards containing instructions on what to invent: for instance "a sad melody", "a bright march", "a syncopated riff", "a tune from an advert" etc.

Further study

There are a number of pieces whose order depends on chance elements, such as the throw of dice. John Cage, whose music is most given to this kind of *aleatorism*, tended to use the *I Ching* rather than dice (eg. *Music of Changes*), but the effect is much the same.

There are also many works built up from diverse and incongruous elements, for example some current dance music contains samples from other songs. In classical music, too, such pieces have occurred in the present century: the third movement of Luciano Berio's *Sinfonia* is a patchwork of music quotations, built round the skeleton of the scherzo from Mahler's Second Symphony.

There is also a musical dice game composed by Mozart, the object of which is to construct a short minuet: each bar is chosen from six alternatives by the throw of a die.

2 Musical sentences

This activity explores the formation of musical sentences by the pairing of phrases. It aims to show how one phrase may complement another.

Preparation

Some work must already have been done on the construction of melodic phrases — see Activity 5 (if not Activity 11) of *Pitch and Melody*.

This activity uses cards prepared as follows. Select pairs of musical phrases, transposing them into the same key (if necessary) and including some minor key examples. The phrase pairs should be symmetrical — each half being 2, 4, 6 or 8 bars in length. Write each phrase on a separate card. You will need at least as many pairs of cards as there will be pairs of students in the class.

The notation used should be adapted to the students' abilities in this field. Graphic notation could be employed for all or some of the card pairs, or simply as a separate, preliminary exercise. Traditional notation can be used without time and/or key signatures. Where students are unsure of traditional notation, cards using it can still be used as an *aide memoire*, if the phrase halves are learnt using the *Copycat* method (Activities 3 and 4 of *Pitch and Melody*). Pitch numbers and Tonic Solfa should also be considered as additions or alternatives.

The pairs opposite should serve as examples.

Instruments must be provided for the activity, unless *D* is sung.

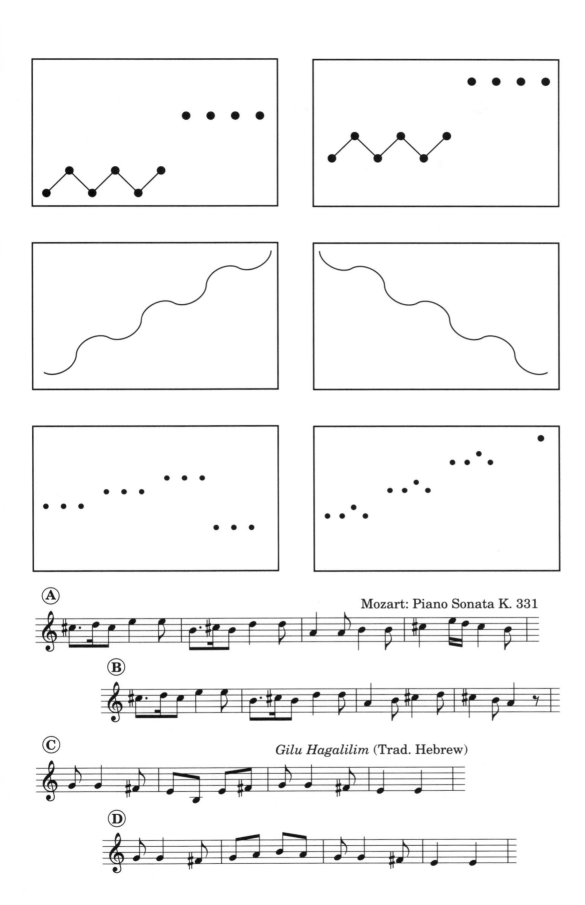

Procedure

A Divide the class into pairs.

B Put one card from each pair of cards in a central position and distribute the others amongst the student pairs.

C Get the student pairs to find the matching card for their phrase, and then to decide on the proper order for the two phrases.

D When all the phrases have been paired, get each student team in turn to sing/play through them, and to tell the remaining students why they think the phrases go together.

E Make a list of all the reasons given under *D*. How many of the following are mentioned as factors relating the two phrases?:

– melodic sequence	– melodic variation
– varied repetition	– exact repetition
– contrasting idea	– same rhythms (different pitches)
– consistent style	– balanced shape
– same time signature	– both have upbeats
– same key (major/minor)	– same pitch range/register
– same length	etc . . .

Variations and extensions

i) Activity 3 forms an extension to the present activity, exploring the grouping of sentences.

ii) Give the students a opening phrase and get them to write a complementary phrase, bearing in mind all the points raised under *E* above.

iii) Contrast symmetrical and asymmetrical phrases. For example, see tunes 57 and 63 in the *Pentatonic Songbook* edited by Brocklehurst (Schott). These show that traditional tunes need not obey the general tendency to balance in phrases of equal length.

iv) Get the students to harmonise the phrases. What cadences are implied?

Further study

Balanced phrases of this kind abound in the music of Haydn and Mozart, recordings of which should provide many clear examples. But is also possible to find asymmetrical phrases there, such as the seven (3 + 4) bars opening the overture to Mozart's *The Marriage of Figaro*.

Blues pieces often have pairs of two-bar phrases balanced in a question-and-answer manner (see Activity 5 of *Pitch and Melody*).

3 Musical paragraphs

This activity follows up Activity 2 and explores how sentences may be grouped together to form a musical paragraph.

Preparation

This activity calls for prepared cards. These are exactly as in Activity 2, but instead of pairs of phrase cards, sets of four are required. In each case, the four phrases making up each set must add up to a complete paragraph consisting of two sentence pairs. The phrase lengths should be equal, and they should be written without a key or time-signature. It follows that you will need at least as many sets of four cards as there are *pairs* of students. The following phrases should serve as examples:

Order and grouping of phrases:

1. A E G M - Somerset folk song *The Streams of Lovely Nancy*
2. B F J P - Mozart aria *Deh vieni, non tardar (Marriage of Figaro)*
3. C H O L - Hungarian Peasant Song
4. D N K I - Chinese song *River Chang Jiang*

Instruments will be required for the activity, unless *C* is sung.

Procedure

A Divide the class into pairs.

B Distribute one card from each set of four to each student pair, instructing them to find the three related phrases and then to decide on the correct order for the set of four. Set an agreed time limit.

C As in the previous activity, get the student pairs in turn to perform their phrases, and to explain i) how they chose the remaining three phrases and ii) how they decided on their order. Again, you may find it helpful to make a list of the reasons given by the students.

D Discuss the inter-relationship of phrases within each group of four. Where appropriate, give each phrase a letter to construct a model of the relationship, for instance A B A C, or A B^1 C B^2.

Variations and extensions

i) Get the students to make up a musical paragraph of this kind from four related phrases of their own invention.

ii) Analyse folk songs (with verse-only structures), using the methods outlined in *D* above. This is a useful preliminary exercise to the following activity.

iii) As an alternative to *B*, distribute one card to each student and ask them to find the other students who hold the matching cards in each set.

Further study

See the corresponding section of the previous activity.

4 Song form 1 — verse structures

In this activity students compose four phrases to fit a given set of verse lyrics.

Preparation

Some preliminary work is advisable on word rhythms (for instance, Activities 7 and 8 of *Rhythm and Metre*) and the harmonisation of melodies (for instance, Activities 5, 7, 8 and 10 of *Harmony*).

The ancillary sections require:
- sheet music of multiple settings of the text quoted under *A* [suggestions under var.i)]
- alternative text(s) [var.ii)]

Procedure

A Get the students, in groups, to scan the first verse of the traditional Somerset folk-song *Geordie*, marking the main accents:

> Come bridle me my milk white steed,
> Come bridle me my pony,
> That I may ride to fair London town
> To plead for my Geordie.

(There are a further five verses, verse 2 being quoted under *Discussion points* below.)

B Get each group to decide on a time signature and then, separately, to rehearse reciting the words against a steady beat.

C The groups in turn perform their versions of the text.

D Get the class to discuss the different versions.

E Get the students, individually or in pairs, to choose a key and write four melodic phrases to fit the rhythmic and lyrical structure of the words.

F Get the students in turn to sing/play their melodies to the class.

G Discuss the melodies and phrase structures, as well as the effectiveness of the melodic contour in bringing out the meaning of the words.

H Get the students, in groups, to write chord progressions to go with selected melodies.

I Perform the resulting compositions in turn, and discuss.

Variations and extensions

i) Play through and discuss some traditional settings of these lyrics. See, for instance, No.9 in *100 English Folksongs* edited by Cecil Sharp (reprinted by Dover Publications) and No.16B in *Traveller's Songs from England and Scotland* by E. MacColl and P. Seeger (Routledge and Kegan Paul).

ii) Use different lyrics for the activity, taken from one of the publications just mentioned.

iii) Write down the rhythms of the versions from *C* and/or the rhythms and pitches of the melodies from *F*.

Discussion points

– How far are the melodic and rhythmic phrases devised for the first verse suitable also for the second verse:

> And when she entered in the hall,
> There were lords and ladies plenty
> Down on her knees she then did fall
> To plead for the life of Geordie.

– How far does the repetition of words in the final line of verse suggest the use of a refrain?

Further study

Popular songs which provide good examples of verse-only structures are Stevie Wonder's *All is fair in love* and *Never dreamed you'd leave in summer*. Clear verse structures are also to be found in Lennon and McCartney's *Let it Be* and *Day Tripper* and Paul Simon's *Bridge over troubled water*; but it is important in these cases to avoid confusing the issue with the refrain sections.

5 Introductions and codas

This activity aims to explore the use and effect of introductions and codas.

Preparation

This activity calls for sheet music and/or commercial recordings of music with clear examples of introductions and codas [suggestions under *C*, and *Further study*].

Procedure

A Get the class to name any pieces they can think of with a memorable introduction or ending.

B In addition (or alternatively) play through some introductions and codas to well-known pieces. For instance, the introductions to Sousa's march *Liberty Bell* (used by the *Monty Python* series):

or to the Wedding March from Mendelssohn's music to *A midsummer night's dream*:

Or these popular closing "tags":

C Discuss these examples and the possible reasons for pieces of music to have introductions and codas.

D Get the students to consider what contribution the piano's introduction and coda make to the effectiveness of Schumann's song *Im wunderschönen Monat Mai* (from the *Dichterliebe* cycle, Op.48):

Langsam, zart.
Adagio, dolce.

Mai,   als al - le Vö - gel san - gen,   da
May,   *When all the birds were sing - ing,*   *I*

20

hab' ich ihr ge - stan - den   mein Seh - nen und Ver-
stood be - fore my true love   *My yearn - ing to her*

25

lan - gen.
bring - ing.

ri - tar - dan - do

Ped.   ✻

E Where appropriate, get the students to write introductions and/or codas to the folk-song settings they composed in the previous activity.

Variations and extensions

i) Analyse the phrase structure of the Schumann song.

ii) Further work is done with introductions in Activities 9 and 12. Introductions appear in Ensemble Pieces Nos.5, 9, 10, 11 and 12 (found in the *Ensemble Scores* volume).

Discussion points

– Which introductions and codas use ideas from the rest of the piece and which are entirely distinct?

Further study

Amongst popular songs, there are noteworthy introductions to Masser and Creed's *The greatest love of all* and Stevie Wonder's *You are the sunshine of my life*, with its use of whole-tones. The "fade-out" coda is a commonplace of the pop song, but several numbers by the Beatles had extended and significant codas — amongst them, *Strawberry Fields*, *All you need is love*, *Hello Goodbye*, *I am the Walrus*, *I Want You* (*She's so heavy*): in the case of *Hey Jude*, the coda was actually longer than the rest of the song.

In the field of classical music, some of the clearest introductions occur in the slow introductions to symphonies by Haydn (eg. Nos.84–86, 88, 90–94, and 96–104), Mozart (Nos.36, 38 and 39) and Beethoven (Nos.1, 2, 4, 7 and 9). Often introductions, especially to longer pieces such as operas or oratorios, grew to complete movements — overtures/preludes. Some introductions have become famous in their own right, and are much better known than the pieces they introduce — Tchaikovsky's First Piano Concerto and Richard Strauss' *Also sprach Zarathustra* are cases in point. The extended introduction to Dohnányi's *Variations on a nursery song* makes many oblique references to fragments of its theme: the students might be asked to guess the tune it is based on.

6 Two-part round

In this activity, students invent a two-part round, first as a whole class under the direction of the teacher, then in smaller groups.

Preparation

Some work must already have been done on scales and triads — see Activities 3, 4, 7, 9 and 10 of *Pitch and Melody* and Activities 2/3 of *Harmony*.

This activity calls for:
– blackboard (with staves)
– tape recorder
– instruments (unless *D*, *F*, *G* and *J* are all sung)

Procedure

A Get the class to choose a time signature and a scale. The scale should be either pentatonic or major, the latter using only *do→so* (including the lower *so,*).

B Get the class to construct an eight-bar melody, made up of two complementary four-bar phrases. Each bar must begin with a note drawn from the tonic triad (I), and the melody (in the first instance) should use only minims and crotchets.

C As the melody develops, write it down on a blackboard stave (or similar), with the four bars of each phrase aligned vertically. The result should be along the lines of:

2nd group starts → **

D Get the class to sing/play the completed melody and make any improvements that seem called for.

E Divide the class into two groups.

F Get the two groups to perform the melody as a round: the first group begins and the second group enters when the first has reached bar 5. Each group sings/plays through the melody a given number of times without pausing in between.

G When performance as a round causes no problems, repeat *F*, making a tape recording.

H Get the class to listen to the recording and identify where clashes and doublings occur.

I Help the class adjust the melody to their satisfaction, reminding them that some clashes and doublings may be appropriate to the character of the piece and others so transitory as to be insignificant.

J Perform/record the revised round, and discuss why it works.

K Get the students (in smaller groups) to make up their own eight-bar rounds following the same procedure.

Variations and extensions

i) Add simple rhythmic ostinatos to *J*, for instance:

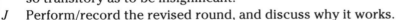

ii) If suitable, perform the revised (*I*) form of the melody as a four-part round, with groups entering at two-bar intervals. (If the class melody proves unsuitable, the example in *C* above might be used instead.) You may want to transpose one or more of the parts up or down an octave.

iii) Get the students to write their own rounds down on manuscript paper, with the bars of the second phrase exactly aligned beneath those of the first. This method should reveal any problems of clashes or doubling.

iv) Perform a two-part round in a minor key, such as the traditional *Shalom*:

Sha - lom my—friend sha - lom my— friend sha - lom   sha - lom

2nd group
starts → **

un - til   we— meet a - gain my— friend sha - lom   sha - lom.

■ Activities 7–12

AIMS
1 To explore imitative structures further.
2 To explore simple ground bass structures.
3 To explore and create a 12-bar blues.
4 To explore simple binary forms.
5 To explore verse and refrain structures

7 Three-part round — By the waters of Babylon

This activity is a follow-up to Activity 6. It involves learning a melody by ear, performing it as a three-part round and analysing its structure.

Preparation

This activity calls for:
– a drum
– a tape recorder

while the ancillary sections require:
– instruments [var.i)]
– commercial recordings [suggestions under *Further study*]

Procedure

A Get one student to establish a duple beat on a drum.

B Teach the following tune by ear, phrase by phrase, to the class. Students should repeat the phrases immediately, without breaking the rhythmic continuity.

By_____ the wa - ters, the wa - ters of Ba - by - lon

We lay down and wept ___ and wept ___ for thee, Zi - on

We re-mem-ber thee, re-mem-ber thee, re-mem-ber thee, Zi - on.

C Repeat the whole tune until secure.

D Divide the class into three groups.

E Perform the piece as a three-part round, groups entering at four-bar intervals and repeating the tune a set number of times.

F When the round is secure, record a performance.

G Play the recording, inviting comments on the construction of the piece. The following observations might be made:

- Phrases 1 and 2 fall in pitch (mainly stepwise), reflecting the mood of the words.
- Phrase 3 also falls overall, though the pitch contour of each bar seems to rise.
- Each phrase contains a rhythmic and melodic sequence.
- The tune is in the minor key throughout — the natural minor (apart from the G♯).
- The melody works as a round because the three phrases are all based on the chord progression — I │♭VII│ VI│ V/I (ie. the chords Am, G, F and E/Am).
- Bars 6, 7 and 8 contain chords with 4–3 suspensions.

Variations and extensions

i) Transfer the round to instruments, adding a rhythmic accompaniment.

ii) Get the students to write their own three-part rounds, using the above as a model. Begin with a chord progression, which each of the three phrases must use as a basis for the melody.

Further study

There is a version of *By the waters of Babylon* by Don MacLean, on his album *American Pie*.

8 Eight-bar ground bass

In this activity, students construct an eight-bar ground bass line and write variations over it.

Preparation

Some work must already have been done on harmony — see Activity 10 of *Harmony*.

Var.i) requires a tape recorder.

Procedure

A   Divide the students into groups.

B   Get each group to select a time signature and major key for the activity.

C   Supply the students with a common four-chord progression, and get each group to construct an eight-bar bass line around it. The chords should change every two bars, and the line use predominantly slow rhythms. For example, the chord progression I–VI–IV–V might result in:

* = passing notes

D   Get each group to sing/play its bass line and to adjust it to taste.

E   In pairs, get one student to sing/play the bass line repeatedly, and the other to invent over it a tune using the same chord progression and slow rhythms, such as:

F   Get the pairs to write down their tune and the bass in score form; this can be used to identify and iron out any problems of clashes or doubling.

G   Get the pairs to compose variations on their tune or to add other parts, still adhering to the bass line and chord sequence. With the bass line repeated, the variations will extend the piece to 16, 24, 32 etc bars.

Variations and extensions

i)   Arrange pieces produced under *G* for ensemble and perform/record the enlarged versions.

ii) Choose one of the bass lines from *D*, and get the class, working in pairs or small groups, to compose tunes and variations over it. Then get the class, working once more as a whole, to assemble all these ideas into an extended piece. Perform/record as in i).

iii) Play any of the finished pieces, beginning with the eight-bar bass line by itself as an introduction. Repeat without this introduction. Which way is better? Why?

Further study

Listen to Ben E. King's *Stand by Me* and note the ground bass:

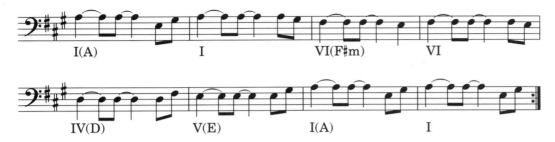

As a form-generating process, the ground bass is mostly confined to classical music, particularly that of the 17th and 18th centuries (or by later composers looking to the past). For clear examples, listen to Dido's arias *When I am laid in earth* (five-bar bass) and *Ah Belinda!* (four-bar), both from Purcell's *Dido and Aeneas*, Monteverdi's *Zefiro torna* (the "ciaccona" from the 1632 *Scherzi musicali*, not the madrigal)(two-bar), the *Crucifixus* from Bach's B minor Mass (four-bar), Bach's C minor Passacaglia (BWV 582) for organ (eight-bar) and the finale of Brahms' Fourth Symphony (eight-bar, adapted from Bach).

The straight-jacket of the repeated bass line made it difficult for composers to construct pieces of any reasonable length. It became more usual to base variational works of this kind on the chord sequence alone, and this is the technique behind most sets of closed variations. It is also found in jazz and pop, particularly in the immense repertory based on the 12-bar blues sequence, which forms the subject of the next activity.

9 12-bar blues — structure

In this activity the class examines the main structural elements of a song based on the standard 12-bar blues. This forms a preliminary to Activity 10 where such a song is composed to a given lyric.

Preparation

This activity calls for a commercial recording of a song based on the standard 12-bar blues (suggestion under *A*).

Procedure

A   Play a recording of a standard 12-bar blues number, such as *Sorry Feeling Blues* from the album *The story of the blues* (CBS 22135), and ask the students to write down comments under various headings (melody; rhythm; instrumentation; chord structure; lyric structure and content).

2nd Verse

I went home last night, I had to be there alone,
I went home last night, I had to be there alone,
Lord I felt for my baby, mmm she was gone.

3rd Verse

Baby, I may never see your face again
Baby, I may never see your face again
But you always must say, I really have been your friend.

Solo guitar over verse

4th Verse

Mmm some of these days, baby, I know it won't be long
Mmm some of these days, baby, I know it won't be long
You're going to want for me, baby, but you will be gone.

5th Verse

Ev'ry time I go home now, I miss you more and more,
Ev'ry time I go home now, I miss you more and more,
I believe you misses me, but you hate to tell me so.

B Discuss the points noted, replaying the recording as appropriate. The following points may emerge:

- There is a 12-bar repeating structure, built on three four-bar sentences.
- The first and second sentences are alike or very similar, while the third differs both melodically and lyrically.
- The melodies are often based on the blues minor scale, with the melody notes sometimes clashing with the harmony underneath. Hence the term "blue notes" — the minor third of the blues scale clashes with the major third in the chord. The "blue notes" are sometimes performed as microtones, somewhere between the exact major and minor thirds.
- The melody of the second and subsequent verses is the same as the first (or very nearly).
- The time signature: most blues are in quadruple time ($\frac{4}{4}$ or $\frac{12}{8}$).
- The rhythms of the melodic line are frequently syncopated and anticipate the beat. Often they contain dotted or "swung" rhythms.
- In most cases, each four-bar sentence consists of a two-bar vocal phrase followed by a two-bar instrumental phrase, often in a question-and-answer manner.
- The key is usually major, with the harmony based on the 12-bar sequence: I I I I IV IV I I V IV I I (or V). The chords are often decorated by 7ths; in more recent pieces 6ths and 9ths may also be used.
- Frequently the lyrics tell a sad story or express discontent. Usually the first and second lines are identical, while the third forms a contrast.
- Instrumentation. The instrumentation varies according to the type of blues. Early rural blues songs were usually performed vocally with acoustic guitar accompaniment; they may, however, contain guitar solos and changes of guitar figuration. More recent urban blues (especially rhythm-and-blues pieces) were written for band performance by electric guitars, keyboards, drums, harmonica, brass instruments etc. In such cases, songs may contain more solos and changes in accompaniment patterns, sometimes quite sophisticated ones.
- Introduction: it is common for blues songs to have an introduction, using, for instance, the last four bars of the cycle.

10 12-Bar blues — making a melody

In this activity students invent melodies for a given set of blues lyrics.

Preparation

Some work must already have been done on the pentatonic minor scale (Activity 9 of *Pitch and Melody*) on the basic chord structure of the 12-bar blues (Activity 9 of *Harmony*) and on the overall structure of a 12-bar blues song (see previous Activity). Revise these as necessary.

This activity calls for:
- blues lyrics (example provided)
- instruments (for harmonic work)

Procedure

A Give the students a set of blues lyrics, such as the author's *The drinkin' man's blues*:

> *My baby left me, she took the mornin' train,*
> *My baby left me, she took the mornin' train,*
> *I swear I'll keep drinkin' till she comes back again.*
>
> *She said she don't love me, can't live here no more,*
> *She said she don't love me, can't live here no more,*
> *Just packed her bags, walked straight out the door.*
>
> *Please believe me, I didn't mean to treat you bad,*
> *Please believe me, I didn't mean to treat you bad,*
> *Cos', baby, you's the best thing I ever had.*
>
> *So I'm sittin' here drinkin' my whole life away,*
> *So I'm sittin' here drinkin' my whole life away,*
> *My baby left me, long before the break of day.*

B Get the students to scan the words and mark the accented syllables for the first verse.

C Get the students (in groups) to invent a melody to go with the lyrics of the first verse. The rhythms should reflect the natural word stresses identified in *B*, and the phrase structure should conform to the pattern covered in the previous activity (Activity 9). It may be easiest for the students of each group to take turns improvising blues melodies (using notes from the minor pentatonic scale) whilst the others play through the chord sequence.

D When all the groups have agreed on their chosen melody, get them to rehearse until all their members can sing (or, if necessary, play) it.

E Get each group to devise an accompaniment for its melody and rehearse this.

F Perform each piece in turn.

G Discuss.

Variations and extensions

i) Use alternative lyrics, such as Chuck Berry's *School Days*.

ii) Get the students to write their own lyrics to the same plan: two identical lines followed by a contrasting third. [This could be pursued as a joint project with the English department.]

iii) Use a variation of the chord scheme — see Activities 15 and 21 of *Harmony*.

iv) Structure the piece by varying the accompaniment pattern for each verse. For instance, use nothing but first-beat cut chords for one verse.

Discussion points

– How many of the features noted in Activity 9 are contained in these blues settings?

11 Simple binary form

This activity explores simple two-part structures. Students examine an Irish hornpipe and use this as a model to create their own examples.

Preparation

This activity calls for cards each containing a phrase from a chosen Irish hornpipe. For instance, the hornpipe known as *The Greencastle*:

requires eight cards, each containing a two-bar phrase. The cards must be large enough for their content to be seen by the whole class.

Further examples of hornpipes may be found in *The Irish Fiddler*, published by Mozart Allan.

Procedure

A   Play the phrases of the chosen hornpipe to the class in random order, with the corresponding card displayed in each case.

B   Get the class to determine the correct order of the phrases.

C   When this has been achieved, analyse the structure of the hornpipe in question. The following account of *The Greencastle* will serve as an example:

Sections:	A	B
No. of bars:	8 repeated	8 repeated
Phrases:	a¹(2) a²(2) a¹(2) b(2)	c¹(2) c²(2) d(4)
Main cadences:	Imperfect/perffect	Perfect/perfect
Keys:	G major	[Em] [Dmaj] G maj
Other features:	Upbeats to phrases.	Phrases c¹ and c² are
	Phrase a¹ is repeated	related by sequence.
	and a² begins as a¹.	Phrase d ends as b.
	Triadic contours.	Stepwise melodic movement.
	Dotted rhythms and	Higher pitch range.
	triplets in $\frac{4}{4}$ time	

(The use of a¹, a² etc, indicates phrases which are closely related, but not exact repeats.)

D   Get the students (individually or in pairs) to write their own hornpipes, using the scheme arrived at in *C* as a model.

E   Perform and discuss the resulting compositions.

Variations and extensions

i)   Contrast your chosen hornpipe with the *Hornpipe* from Handel's *Water Music*:

Make a list of the differences and similarities. In particular, notice the modulation to the dominant key at the end of the first section, and the return to the tonic key at the end of the second section.

ii)   Get the students to write a modulating binary piece modelled on Handel's structure.

Further study

Simple binary form of this kind is used in dance suites of the baroque era, many examples of which can be found in commercial recordings. It was also occasionally used later, for instance by the theme of the second movement of Haydn's Symphony No.94 (*Surprise*).

Further work on binary form is done in Activity 13, which introduces asymmetrical binary structures. Activity 20 of *Rhythm and Metre* includes the jig *The Irish Washerwoman*.

12 Song form 2 – verse and chorus structures

This activity explores the verse/chorus structure common in songs as an extension of the binary form of the previous activity.

Preparation

This activity calls for commercial recordings of songs with a simple verse/chorus pattern (suggestions under A), while the ancillary var.i) requires verse/chorus lyrics for student settings (sources suggested).

Procedure

A Play recordings of songs with a simple verse/chorus structure, asking the students to note the points which differentiate chorus from verse. Examples from classical music include Dowland's lute songs (for instance *Come again, sweet love doth now invite* from his *First Booke of Songes or Ayres*) and from amongst popular songs Bob Marley's *One Love*, Elvis Costello's *Alison* and Lennon and McCartney's *Get Back*.

B Make a list of the points noted, which may include: the verse lyrics change whereas the chorus lyrics do not; choruses tend to have the more catchy tunes and lyrics (hooklines) and so on.

C Choose one song for a more detailed analysis of overall structure and phrase structure. The following example is based on Stevie Wonder's *You are the sunshine of my life* (on the albums *Talking Book* and *Original Musiquarium 1*):

Sections:		‖: A	B	:‖ A
	Intro	Chorus	Verse	Chorus
No. of bars:	4	16	16	16
Phrases:	a	b c^1 b c^2	d^1 d^2 d^3 e	*as before*
Main cadences:	Imperfect	Perfect/perfect	Perfect/Imperfect	
Keys:	B♭ major	B♭ major	B♭ major (G) B♭	B major

(The use of c^1, c^2 etc, indicates phrases which are closely related, but not exact repeats.)

D Liken this alternation of chorus/verse to an extension of simple binary form.

Variations and extensions

i) Give the students some verse/chorus lyrics to set. Good examples are provided by some of the less well-known Beatles lyrics (in *The Beatles Complete*) or by songs from Tin Pan Alley, published in various compilations by Chappell.

ii) Get the students to name any examples of verse/chorus songs they can think of.

Activities 13–18

> **AIMS**
> 1 To explore extended binary forms.
> 2 To explore theme and variation forms.
> 3 To explore ternary forms.
> 4 To explore the use of bridge sections in song forms.
> 5 To explore larger structures in which two forms are combined.

13 Asymmetrical binary form

This activity explores binary structures in which the second section is longer than the first. It forms a follow-up to Activity 11.

Preparation

This activity calls for:

– a commercial recording of (the *Bourrée* and *Hornpipe* from) Handel's *Water Music*
– score(s) of the *Bourrée* or phrase cards [see *B*]

Procedure

A Revise Activity 11, including var.i) with its discussion of Handel's *Hornpipe*.

B Play a recording of the *Bourrée* from Handel's *Water Music*, getting the students (if possible) to follow the score:

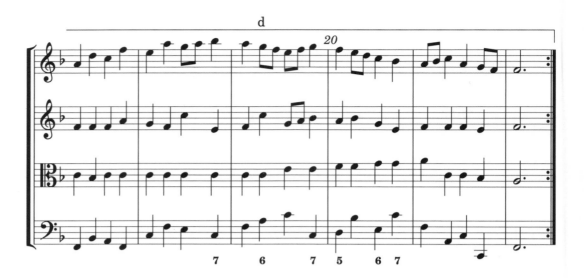

(If this is not possible, make phrase cards of the melodic line, and get the students to determine their correct order, as in Activity 11.)

C   Get the class to analyse the structure of the piece, producing a map covering such points as phrase structure, main cadence points, key changes etc. The following may serve as a model:

Sections:	‖: A¹ :‖	‖: B A² :‖

No. of bars:	8 repeated	8 repeated
Phrases structure:	a (4) b (4)	c (8) d (6)
Main cadences:	Perfect/perfect	Perfect/perfect
Keys:	F → C	C (Dm) (Gm) F

Other features
– the melody is characterised by rising leaps of a fourth, followed by falling seconds.
– the phrases all begin with upbeats.
– phrase c begins as phrase a, but in the dominant key.
– phrase d begins with a repeat of phrase a in the tonic key, but ends with new material in stepwise movement.
– harmony of bars 12–15 uses the cycle of 5ths with a sequential melodic figure.

D   Get the students to write their own melodic phrases in asymmetrical binary form, using the map of the Handel as a model.

Variations and extensions

i)   Get the students to replace the B section in the above plan (ie. phrase c) with the following more extended model:
– repeat phrase a in the dominant key
– add new phrases c and d using sequences and modulations [substantially the same as the complete original B section]
– add phrase b2, ending with the close of phrase b in the tonic key

ii) Get the students to compose binary pieces in which the sections are contrasted in other ways: instrumentally, stylistically, metrically etc.

Further study

By far the most ready source of asymmetrical binary forms remains the baroque dance suite. This form, however, is the basis of the minuet and trio, as used throughout the 18th and 19th centuries: the minuet of Beethoven's Symphony No.1, for instance, with its 8-bar A section and 71-bar B section is nothing if not asymmetrical.

14 Theme and variations

This activity explores theme and variation structures, which have been widely used in the classical music of the last 300 years and are also found in jazz pieces.

Preparation

Some work must have been done on the transcription of melodies using pitch numbers (see Activity 3 of *Pitch and Melody*) and on harmonising with primary chords (see Activity 8 of *Harmony*).

Procedure

A Choose a simple melody to be used as a theme, for instance the chorus of the traditional gospel song *When the saints go marching in*.

B Get the students to work out the melody using pitch numbers or solfa and add the rhythm. In the case of our example:

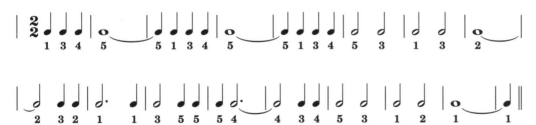

C Get the students to harmonise the tune simply, using the primary chords I, IV and V.

D Through class discussion make a list of the ways a theme can be varied, for instance:
  – by changing some of the pitches e.g. by inversion, retrograde etc.
  – by adding ornaments/decorations
  – by changing the metre and/or some of the rhythms and/or the tempo
  – by changing the expression through use of dynamics, accents, rubato etc.
  – by changing the harmony and/or the key (from major to minor, for instance)
  – by using the harmonic plan of the theme as the basis for a different melody (as with the ground bass variations)
  – by taking one or two motifs from the melody and composing a contrasting piece using them.
  – by changing the instrumentation and timbre (*pizz/arco*; muted etc.).

E Invent and play some variations (or at least variation openings) to illustrate each of the techniques identified in *D*. The following examples are based on the first phrase:

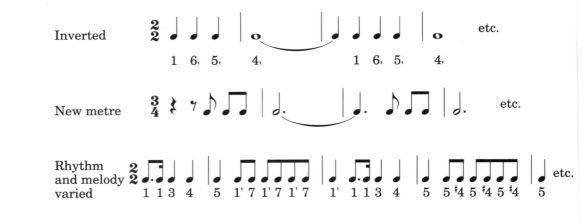

Inverted

1 6, 5,   4,   1 6, 5,   4,   etc.

New metre

etc.

Rhythm
and melody
varied

1 1 3 4   5 1' 7 1' 7 1' 7   1' 1 1 3 4   5 5 ♮4 5 ♮4 5 ♮4   5   etc.

F   Get the students individually to write a set of four variations on a theme.
G   Perform the results of *F* in turn.

Variations and extensions

i)   Arrange the results of *F* for ensemble and perform.
ii) As an alternative theme, use the Spanish tune *La folia*:

Anon.

1st time   2nd time

iii) Set the whole class the same theme as for *F*. Then get the students to construct a
     longer set of variations from their contributions.

Discussion points

– What qualities make the best kind of theme for variational treatment?
– How are variations linked together in a piece? What governs the order in which they
   appear?

Further study

In the field of jazz, variation form was often used in the New Orleans and Chicago style,
for instance in Louis Armstrong's *Cornet Chop Suey*, and recordings of *When the saints
go marching in*.
    Of the many examples of variation form in classical music, the following illustrate
some particular point.

i)   variations on the same theme by composers of widely different styles

     Two themes stand out here. First is *La folia*, quoted in var.ii) above, which was used
     by C.P.E. Bach (12 variations for keyboard), Domenico Scarlatti (*Variazioni sulla
     Follia di Spagna*), Corelli (Violin Sonata, Op.5 No.12), Vivaldi (Trio Sonata Op. 1 No.
     12, *La Follia*), Gaspar Sanz (Spanish Suite for guitar), Liszt (*Spanish Rhapsody* for
     piano) and Rakhmaninov (Variations for piano on a theme of Corelli, Op.42). The
     second is the famous Paganini theme, used for variations by Paganini himself

(Caprice for violin, Op.1 No.24), Liszt (Paganini Study No.6 for piano), Brahms (Studies for piano, Op.35 — two books), Rakhmaninov (Rhapsody for piano and orchestra, Op.43), Lutoslawski (Variations for two pianos), Boris Blacher (Variations for orchestra) and Andrew Lloyd Webber (Variations). Of these the Liszt and Lutoslawski are noteworthy in that they not only use Paganini's theme, but also "rework" each of Paganini's variations in their own terms.

ii) variations on famous themes

Beethoven wrote piano variations on both *God save the king* and *Rule Britannia*: Charles Ives also produced a set of variations for organ on the first of these, under its alternative name *God bless America*. There are variations on the nursery song *Twinkle, twinkle, little star* by Mozart (*Ah, vous dirai-je, maman*, K.265 for piano) and Dohnányi (for piano and orchestra, Op.25). Haydn used variations on his own *Emperor's Hymn* (better known as the former German national anthem, *Deutschland über alles*) as the slow movement of his String Quartet in C, Op.76 No.3. In the same category can be considered the fourth movement of Schubert's *Trout* Quintet, with its variations on Schubert's own song *Die Forelle*.

iii) variations of instrumentation and timbre only

Two orchestral pieces in particular epitomise this technique — Ravel's *Bolero* and Glinka's *Kamarinskaya*.

15 Ternary form

This activity introduces and explores ternary form structures.

Procedure

A Get the class to play through *Ensemble Piece No.7*, a "Ballet" taken from Praetorius' collection *Terpsichore*. The score is in the *Ensemble Scores* volume and the parts can be found in Unit 15 of the instrumental workbooks.

B Analyse the structure of the piece using headings similar to those used in Activities 9, 11, 12 and 13.

C Produce a structural map, as in those activities. For instance:

	Section A	Section B	Section A
No. of bars:	16	16	R E
Phrases: (all 4 bars)	$a^1\ b^1\ a^2\ b^2$	$c^1\ d^1\ c^2\ d^2$	P E A
Main cadences:	Impf/Pf/Impf/Pf/	Impf/Pf*/Impf/Pf*	T E
Keys:	G major	(B♭) G minor	D

Other features

– In both sections the second sentence is a decoration of the first: it is also played by solo instruments, providing a contrasting texture.

– Phrase c¹ contains melodic sequences.
    Pf* = perfect cadence with *tierce de Picardie*

D   Get the students to compose their own ternary form piece, using the structure revealed in *B/C* as a model.

Variations and extensions

i)   Get the students to use some of the (more cosmetic) variation techniques used in the previous activity to vary the repetitions of phrases and sections in their pieces.

ii) Activity 18 forms an extension of the present one, combining and superimposing binary and ternary forms.

Further study

Ternary form structures are used by music from a wide range of cultures, ranging from contemporary African pieces, such as Salif Keita's *Soro (Afriki)*, through Irish reels, such as *The Rising Sun or Morning Star*, to jazz pieces, such as Duke Ellington's *Janet* from the album *The Duke plays Ellington* (in which the moods of the lady are reflected in each section).

In classical music, ternary form is especially common amongst shorter pieces (typically 2–4 minutes in length) of the last 200 years, short genre pieces for piano and the like.

Ternary form is also closely related to the *Da capo aria* form of the baroque period, where a piece would consist of two contrasting sections (AB) and end with the instruction to repeat the first of these: as the name suggests, this was particularly prevalent in opera and oratorio (often to show a character's conflicting emotions — sorrow/anger/sorrow), but examples are also found in instrumental music, notably in the first movement of Bach's E major Violin Concerto.

16 Song form 3 — the bridge

This activity explores the function within a song structure of a bridge section.

Preparation

This activity calls for commercial recordings of songs with clear bridge sections — suggestions under *C* and var.i).

Procedure

A   Play the class a song containing a clear bridge section.

B   Get the class to analyse the structure in the way familiar from previous activities.

C   From these discussions, produce a structural map such as the following, which is based on Paul Simon's *Still crazy after all these years* from the album of the same name. (It is not anticipated that the fine details of the following structural analysis will be covered. Rather, students should be encouraged to identify the *main* structural divisions and concentrate on the volume of a bridge section.)

	Intro	Verse 1 and refrain	V2 & r	Bridge	Solo	Verse 3 and refrain
No. of bars:	8	12 + 11		29	16	12 + 12
Phrases: (bars in brackets)	a' b (3) (5)	c d e f¹ f² g (4)(4)(4)(3)(4)(4)		a² h a³ a⁴x8 (4)(4)(5) (2)	j k (8)(8)	Repeat of verse 1 with varied refrain
Main cadences:		Pf Int Pf			Pl*	Int / Pf
Keys:	G major	→		[E F♯ C] Am A	G	A A

	Intro	Verse 1 and refrain	V2 & r	Bridge	Solo	Verse 3 and refrain
Phrases: (bars in brackets)	a' b (3)(5)	c d e f^1 f^2 g (4)(4)(4)(3)(4)(4)		a^2 h a^3 a^4x8 (4)(4)(5)(2)	j k (8)(8)	Repeat of verse 1 with varied refrain

Other features
- upbeats to verse phrases.
- melodic phrases mostly pentatonic.
- bridge develops ideas from the Intro.

Pl* = plagal (here II^7 — I)

D Discuss the functions of the bridge section. In the Paul Simon example above the bridge:
- has a developmental function, taking material from the introduction and using it in different ways
- introduces new instrumental textures, leading to a saxophone solo
- has, in common with many other bridges, a fluid key scheme, but prepares the key change at the beginning of the solo

E Get the students to rework the songs produced in Activity 12 to include a bridge passage.

Variations and extensions

i) The following songs possess clear bridge sections and could be used instead of/in addition to the above, or as related listening:
- Billy Joel's *My Life*, *She's always a woman to me* and *Just the way you are*
- Burke and Garner's jazz classic *Misty*
- Stephen Sondheim's *Send in the clowns*
- Al Stewart's *The year of the cat*
- Lloyd-Webber and Nunn's *Memory* (from *Cats*), which contains a modulatory bridge

17 Combined forms 1 — ground and round

This activity explores the combination of two forms already covered — the ground bass of Activity 8 and the round of Activities 6 and 7.

Preparation

Var.ii) requires a recording of Pachelbel's Canon for 3 violins and continuo.

Procedure

A Play the students the following simple ground bass theme, asking them to identify the pitches using note names, pitch numbers or Tonic Solfa. For the origin of the following example, see *Historical note* below

B Get the students (individually or in small groups) to construct a two-part round over this bass, using the chord sequence indicated. The parts should move slowly, with long note values. (Only the first four bars of the bass should be used: bars 5–8 are merely a repeat and bar 9 a final tonic to end a piece.) For example:

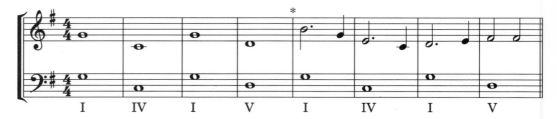

C Perform and discuss the resulting pieces.
D Get the students to add two further parts to the round. These should work harmonically with the others and with the bass, which is played throughout. These phrases should move more quickly, with shorter note values. For example:

* = entry points

E Perform and discuss the four-part versions.

Variations and extensions

i) Adapt the same technique to produce a two-part canon above the bass. The student should use manuscript paper with staves braced into systems of three. In the first four-bar phrase, only the bass is played. In bars 5–8, one part only should be written into Player 1's part: this same phrase is copied into Player 2's part for bars 9–12. A new phrase is invented for Player 1 in bars 9–12, a phrase which must match Player 2's music, the bass line and the chord scheme: this same phrase is copied into Player 2's part for bars 13–16. The piece continues in this way, every four-bar phrase being composed anew for Player 1 and copied by Player 2 in the next four bars, in the pattern:

Player 1:	A	B	C	D	E	→	→	last	silence
Player 2:	–	A	B	C	D	E	→	→	last
bars:	5–8	9–12	13–16	17–20	21–24	25–28	→	final 2	phrases

The plan should be rounded off with a cadence.
ii) Play the students Pachelbel's Canon, getting them to work out the notes of the ground bass theme and first phrases of the canon.

Discussion points

– What difference does the presence of a ground bass make to the round?
– What is the essential difference between a round and a canon?

Historical note

The ground bass and chord sequence quoted in *A* was much used in the renaissance dances popular between 1500 and 1650, such as the *passamezzo moderno*, *quadran pavan*, *villano*, *zarabanda* etc.

18 Combined forms 2 – ternary and binary

This activity explores longer structures which combine binary and ternary forms, in particular a pattern common in ragtime.

Preparation

This activity calls for:
– sheet music and/or commercial recording of a ragtime piece with a clear ABACD structure (examples cited), for analysis
– commercial recordings or sheet music of ragtime pieces, for listening

while the ancillary sections require:
– commercial recordings of minuet and trio movements from the Classical period [see var.i)]
– commercial recordings of ABACD pieces [see var.ii), example cited]

Procedure

A Play the class a ragtime piece with an ABACD structure, such as Scott Joplin's *Maple Leaf Rag*.

B Get the students to make a structural map of the piece in the way familiar from previous activities. The following brief outline of the Joplin example may be useful:

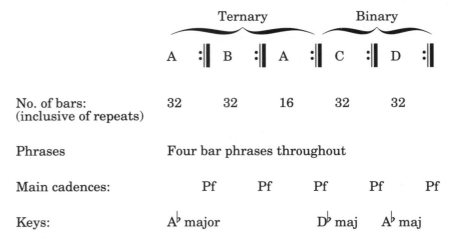

	Ternary			Binary	
	A ‖: B :‖ A		:‖ C	:‖ D :‖	
No. of bars: (inclusive of repeats)	32	32	16	32	32
Phrases	Four bar phrases throughout				
Main cadences:	Pf	Pf	Pf	Pf	Pf
Keys:	A♭ major			D♭ maj	A♭ maj

C Identify this as a binary structure (CD) added to the end of a ternary structure (ABA).
D Play the students further ragtime pieces, asking them to list other characteristics of this genre. These may include:
   – syncopated right hand figures, often with the ⊓⊓⊓ shape, or rhythms tied across a barline or the middle of a bar
   – quaver movement in the left hand harmony
   – "stride" left hand
   – often pentatonic melodies

Variations and extensions

i) Play a minuet and trio movement from a symphony/sonata/quartet etc of the Classical period. Note how this is essentially a ternary arrangement of binary form pieces:

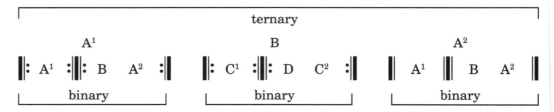

ii) Play any other piece combining binary and ternary form, for instance Sousa's march *Liberty Bell*, with its structure:

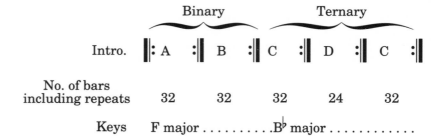

		Binary		Ternary	
Intro.	‖: A :‖	B :‖	C :‖	D :‖	C :‖
No. of bars including repeats	32	32	32	24	32
Keys	F major	B♭ major			

Further study

Other rags with the ABACD structure include Joplin's *The Entertainer* and Scott's *Frogs Legs Rag.*

Activities 19–24

AIMS

1 To explore simple rondo structures.
2 To explore structures based on alternation of solo group and full ensemble sections.
3 To introduce and explore structure in film music.
4 To explore structures used in some Indian music.

19 Simple rondo form

This activity introduces simple rondo form by examining the Gavotte en Rondeau from Bach's Suite for keyboard in G minor, BWV 822, which is then used as a model for student compositions.

Preparation

This activity calls for a commercial recording of the Bach *Gavotte en Rondeau* (unless the teacher or one of the students can perform it) and, if possible, enough copies of the score for the whole class.

Procedure

A   Play the *Gavotte en Rondeau* from Bach's Suite in G minor, BWV 822, asking the students, as in several previous activities, to note down any observations about the structure of the piece, in particular whether any sections are repeated.

Allegretto

B   Compare and discuss the observations.

C   Play just the rondo theme, getting the students to identify the pitches, writing them down in note names, pitch numbers or Tonic Solfa:

(If note names are being used, it might be best to play the theme in A minor — or at least identify the starting note as A.)

D   Analyse with the class the phrase structure of this theme.

E   Play the complete *Gavotte en Rondeau* again, getting the students to make a structural map like those in previous activities. If possible, they should follow the score as they listen. Suggest the use of the term "episode" to designate sections other than the rondo theme.

F   Compare and discuss the student maps, producing a "definitive" map of the piece's structure, which may resemble the following:

Sections:	A	B	A	C	A
Bars:	1–8	9–16	17–24	25–32	33–40
Phrases:		Four bar phrases throughout			
Keys:	G min	B♭ maj. (relative major)	G min	D min (dominant minor)	G min

G   Get the students to produce their own rondo in a minor key, using the definitive map as a model.

Variations and extensions

i)   Organise a play-through of *Ensemble Piece No.5*, a jazz-flavoured rondo in which the episodes are improvised. The score is in the separate *Ensemble Scores* volume; the parts are printed in Unit 11 of the instrumental workbooks which complement this book.

ii)   Get the students to compose rondos in a major key. In classical music, one of the commonest key schemes for a simple rondo in a major key is: **A** (tonic) **B** (dominant) **A** (tonic) **C** (relative minor) **A** (tonic).

iii)   Play other gavottes (such as those from Bach's French Suites Nos.4–6), getting the students to note down stylistic features they have in common.

Further study

There are several clear examples of this form by Purcell, most notably those from the music for *The Fairy Queen* (which uses the key scheme in var.ii) above) and from the music to the play *Abdelazer* (which gave Britten his theme for *The Young Person's Guide to the Orchestra*). It is also used in Jeremiah Clarke's *The Prince of Denmark's March* (long known as 'Purcell's Trumpet Voluntary'). All these pieces were written not long after the form had arrived in this country from Italy and was still known as the *Round O*.

Rondeau is the French spelling: there is a clear example in Rameau's opera *Dardanus* (see LAM 32).

20 Music for film

This activity explores how the film medium imposes its own structural demands on the composer.

Preparation

This activity calls for:
– 2 VCR machines and a television set
– a video of a film clip*
– stopwatches
– instruments

*The film clip is used as the basis of student soundtracks. It should last about 30 seconds, but contain a reasonable amount of incident. The clip should preferably be unfamiliar, to avoid musical preconceptions.

Ideally, you should have an original tape *with* sound and make a number of copies of the clip on to a second tape, all *without* sound. These last will be dubbed with the student soundtracks.

The ancillary sections require:
– a filmscript for a short scene [see var.i)]
– two contrasting filmclips with their soundtracks swapped [see var.ii)]

Procedure

A   Play the class the chosen clip *without* sound, asking the students to make lists of the events in the film in chronological order.

B   When the film is over, get the students to add a note of the mood(s) it creates in their minds. It may be helpful if each student uses a pro forma such as:

Name of video . . . . (a) . . . . Student's name . . . (b) . . . .

Overall mood of the film: (c)

Type of music/style suitable for this mood: (d)

Visual Events	Timings	Musical ideas
1. (e)	(f)	(g)
2. (e)	(f)	(g)
3. etc . . .		

in which case a), b), c) and e) could be filled in at this point.

C   When the lists are complete, get the students to make accurate stopwatch timings of each event on their lists [f] in the sample pro forma] and of the whole clip. (NB It is important that all the students do this because their lists may be different.) Play and repeat the clip as necessary.

D   Get the students to write some ideas for music against each visual event [g]] and to think of an overall musical style suitable for the mood of the whole [d].

E   Get the students (individually or in small groups) to experiment with their musical ideas, making sure that the music fits the image both in mood and in time. For example, if an event recurs, so could the same music; or characters could be given motifs which reappear each time they do.

F   Dub the finished soundtracks on to copies of the clip.

G   Play the versions back and discuss how successful they have been.

H   Play the clip complete with sound and discuss the merits of the original soundtrack.

Variations and extensions

i) Instead of a clip from a film, record a scene devised/scripted and acted by the students themselves. This could be pursued as a joint project with the English or Drama departments.

ii) Take two clips of similar length but contrasting mood and content (for instance a relaxed moment from a comedy and a passage of suspense from a horror film). Swap their soundtracks and discuss the effect.

iii) Listen to the music from a film. Get the students to write down appropriate pictures or scene which might accompany the music.

21 Song form 4 — the Indian ghazal

This activity introduces a popular Indian song form based on Urdu lyric poems called ghazals.

Preparation

This activity requires a recording of a ghazal, for instance *Har Sitam Aap ka* from Najma Akhtar's album *Qareeb* (Triple Earth Records, Terra 003) or Asha Bhosle's *Yuhn Na Thin* on *An Introduction to Asia 1* (Womad 006). In addition, var.i) requires recorded examples of Western operatic arias or songs in which the singers describe their emotions.

Procedure

A   Play the students a ghazal such as Najma Akhtar's *Har Sitam Aap ka*, getting them to write down any observations they have on the structure of the song. One of the most basic points is the alternation of vocal sections and instrumental episodes in an ABABA framework.

B   Look at the lyric structure (notes provided on the record's inner sleeve). Notice that the lines of a ghazal are grouped in couplets. Each couplet is regarded as self-sufficient, expressing a single experience. Like most ghazals, these couplets express feelings of unrequited love. The vocal lines are improvised, the singer attempting to capture the mood of the poem in an intricate decorative style.

The following resumé of *Har Sitam Aap ka* may be useful:

Introduction: an unmeasured slow introduction in which the santoor (a zither-like instrument) and singer introduce the main melodic material. The resemblance to the *alap* section of a raga (see Activity 24) is strong.

Section A: the first couplet, sung three times to a tabla, santoor, electronic keyboard and bass accompaniment (27 bars of slow 44)

Section B: instrumental episode with violin improvisations (11 [5+6] bars)

Section C: the second couplet is sung (16 bars), followed by a double reprise of the first couplet (12 bars)

Section B: instrumental episode (11 bars)

Section D: the third couplet is sung (19 bars), followed by another reprise of the first couplet (6 bars)

Section B: instrumental episode (11 bars)

Section E: the fourth couplet is sung (19 bars), followed by a reprise of the first couplet with a coda using first couplet material (28 bars)

The reprises all use the same music. Each B section uses the same chord sequence, and the improvised violin melodies are quite similar.

The harmony alternates chords of C♯ major (often decorated with 4–3 suspensions) and F♯ minor (often decorated with 9–8 suspensions).

Variations and extensions

i)   Compare Najma Akhtar's recording with Asha Bhosle's *Yuhn Na Thin*.
ii) Compare the expressive qualities of the ghazal with the Western operatic aria or recital song (for instance the German *Lied*).

22 Solo and tutti structures 1 – Voices

This activity examines structures based on alternations of solo voice and chorus.

Preparation

This activity calls for commercial recordings of several pieces based on the alternation of solo voices and chorus. The following types of music could be used:

Unaccompanied vocal

Work songs/sea shanties/field hollers, originally composed to enable a group of people to co-ordinate rhythmic action such as pulling a rope (and sometimes incorporating or imitating the thud of the implement involved), often take the form of solo call and group response. Good examples are provided by *Let your hammer ring* and *Imo Gal* on the album

Black music of two worlds (Folkways FOL/FE 4602). The same pattern is sometimes used by music for the pre-20th century military to march to: the famous Red Army rendition of the folksong *Kalinka* is directly linked to this tradition.

Solo/choral alternation is also a feature: of South African *a cappella*-style singing (for instance the album *Inhala* by Ladysmith Black Mambazo); of various liturgies, in which congregations sing responses to the chanting of a celebrant; and of some negro spirituals such as *One more River* and *Swing low sweet chariot*, both included in *The Pentatonic Songbook* published by Schott.

Similar are pieces based on echo effects, such as Lassus' *Echo Song* (included in the *Penguin Part-Song Book*) in which an echo chorus exchanges ideas with a full chorus.

Accompanied vocal

The dramatic possibilities of solo/chorus alternation has led to many scenes in music theatre pieces, for instance *Mr Mistoffelees* from Lloyd Webber's *Cats* and the "vaudeville" number *Gee, Officer Krupke* from Bernstein and Sondheim's *West Side Story*.

In non-theatre music, there are notable examples in Giovanni Gabrieli's *In ecclesiis* from his *Sacrae Symphoniae* (LAM No.10), in *Circa mea pectora* and *Tempus est iocundum* from Carl Orff's *Carmina Burana*, and in *Humour*, the second movement of Shostakovich's Symphony No.13.

In addition, var.i) calls for song texts or poems.

Procedure

A   Play recordings of pieces based on alternating solo and chorus sections, getting the students to work out the common link between the pieces.

B   Get the students to compose their own pieces containing solo and tutti sections.

Variations and extensions

i)   Give the students song text(s) or poem(s) and ask them to suggest which passages would be suitable for solo and which for choral performance.

ii) The following activity forms a natural extension by exploring instrumental works which contrast solo and ensemble sections.

23 Solo and tutti structures 2 — Instrumental

This activity explores instrumental structures based on the alternation of solo (or solo group) and full ensemble sections. It follows on from the previous activity, which dealt with vocal pieces similarly constituted.

Preparation

This activity calls for commercial recordings of several pieces based on the alternation of solo instrument(s) and a larger group. The following types of music could be used:

South American Carnival Music

In this music, whistles are used to signal in advance the change from one section to another, often preceded by a unison drum beat. Each section tends to feature a particular instrumental group, for instance the *rico-ricos* (scrapers), the friction drums or the tambourims (a type of small tambour played with sticks). Recorded examples may be found on the albums *Dance Mania* by Tito Puente and his orchestra (Carino DBL 1–5017) and *Hits* by Tito Rodrigues (WS-Latino WSLA 4060).

18th-century Concerto Grosso

The concerto grosso contrasted a small solo group (the *concertino*), typically of two violins and cello, with the larger ensemble (the *ripieno*). The concerto would normally start with all the players together, followed by alternations of the *concertino* and *ripieno*. There are many examples by Corelli (for the first movement of his so-called *Christmas Concerto*, Op.6 No.8 see LAM 17) and Vivaldi (for the first movement of the Concerto Op.3 No.11 see LAM 22).

The same idea was used by Bach in the Brandenburg Concertos Nos.1, 2, 4 and 5. Thereafter it lost ground before the solo concerto, though it still resurfaced in such works as Beethoven's Triple Concerto and the Elgar Introduction and Allegro for strings. The second movement of Bartók's Concerto for Orchestra is built round a succession of pairs of instruments.

Solo Concertos

The concerto for a single instrument and orchestra began not long after the concerto grosso and by the late 18th century had almost completely superseded it. The solo concerto could be said to have come of age with the piano concertos of Mozart.

Alternation of a single instrument and a group is found in other fields, notably in jazz, where numbers often take the form of set-piece tuttis interspersed with improvised solos.

Procedure

A   Play recordings of instrumental pieces based on alternating solo and tutti sections, getting the students to work out the common link between the pieces.

B   Revise some of the pieces analysed in previous activities and get the students to suggest which sections would be suitable for solo and which for tutti treatment in an ensemble performance.

24 Raga structures

This activity examines raga structures. Although ragas are improvisatory, they tend to follow certain conventions in the development of their melodic and rhythmic elements.

Preparation

This activity calls for a commercial recording of a raga, and var.i) for a specific such recording.

Procedure

A Play the students the beginning of a recording of a raga, asking them to make a note of the stylistic elements involved.

B Play a passage from near the end of the same raga, again getting the students to note the elements involved.

C From discussion draw out one of the main differences — that the beginning section is unmeasured whilst the end is measured, with its time cycle maintained by the tabla. On a basic level, therefore, the structure can be described as binary.

D Listen to the whole raga, asking the students to write down what features of its sectional form they can discern. A common overall form may be represented as follows:

Unmeasured	Transitional		Measured
Alap	*Johr*	*Jhala*	*Gath*
This introductory section exposes the raga against a drone accompaniment.	These developmental sections gradually introduce rhythmic elements but without the tabla. In the Jhala section the tempo accelerates reaching a fast speed.		This concluding section is fully measured; the tabla introducing a tala. The tempo increases gradually to the end, and rhythmic improvisations become virtuosic.

Variations and extensions

i) Play the students *Raga Mohan Kauns* from *The best of Ravi Shankar and Alla Rakha* (Walkman Classics DG 415 6214) which has the structure outlined under D above. The main structural points are sign-posted by short breaks with glissandos on the treble tanpura. The tala used here is the seven-beat *Rupak*. (NB. This is a long piece (about 25 minutes): students may find difficulty in concentrating if it is played in full.)

Timbre and Texture

CONTENTS

Activities 1–6

1 To explore vocal and instrumental timbres.
2 To develop awareness of, and sensitivity to, timbral contrasts.
3 To explore timbral combinations and simple textures.
4 To develop students' control over timbral parameters.

1 What's in a word

In this activity students experiment with parts of words (beginning sounds, vowel sounds etc.) and make a bank of sounds from which they create group pieces.

Preparation

This activity may call for a prepared list of sounds (see *A*) while the ancillary sections require a composition by the teacher in the style of the activity (var.ii) and prepared flash cards (var.iii and iv).

Procedure

A Through discussion with the class, make out a list of language-related sounds, categorising them according to type. The following should give an idea of the sort of content:

sibilant	rolled "rr"	tip of tongue	vowel	word ends
sh- [**sh**out]	br- [**br**own]	t- [**t**urn]	a [f**a**ther]	-ing [bri**ng**]
ss- [**s**it]	cr- [**cr**own]	d- [**d**irt]	e [c**e**dar]	-ed [end**ed**]
ch- [**ch**ap]	gr- [**gr**een]	j- [**j**et]	i [**i**rate]	-ly [love**ly**]
ph- [**ph**ase]	dr- [**dr**ink]		o [**o**pen]	-er [raid**er**]
			u [l**u**nar]	

You could also do this yourself in advance.

B Select two sounds from different categories.

C Get the class to suggest different ways in which these sounds can be changed, while still remaining recognisably the chosen sound — for instance by varying the dynamic level, attack, duration etc.

D Try these out on the chosen sounds.

E Get the students (working in groups) to select and explore some sounds from this list, experimenting with the order and combination of the sounds. Students could take it in turns to act as conductor, bringing sounds in and out as appropriate.

F Get the groups to build on their experimentation and produce a composition based on their chosen sounds.

G Perform the resulting pieces (recording them, if required for var.i).

Variations and extensions

i) Get the student groups to make graphic scores of the pieces produced under *G*. The groups then exchange graphic scores and perform each other's pieces. Compare the original and new versions of the same pieces, perhaps with the help of tape recordings.

ii) Give the students a similar composition of your own to perform.

iii) Split whole words up into their constituent sounds and use these as the basis of a piece — for instance CH   EE   SE. Your school's name can be very effective in this respect: write the phonemes on flash cards — SS   AI   NT   CH   ARL   ES   SS   CH   OO   L.

iv) Repeat iii), but with three groups independently using the same set of sounds on flash cards. Each group should have its student conductor determining the speed at which the sounds change.

v) Use word sounds to create an abstract or "new" language.

Discussion points

– Which pieces were the most effective? Why?

Further study

For singing that uses voices in an unusual way or phonemes without linguistic sense, the following are recommended:

– *Listen to the rhythm* from Sweet Honey in the Rock's album *We all . . . Everyone of us* (Spindrift SPIN 106)
– "scat singing", most notably in *Oh lady be good* and *How high the moon* from Ella Fitzgerald's album *Best of Ella Fitzgerald* (MCA MCLC 1611)
– Luciano Berio's *Sequenza III*
– Peter Maxwell Davies' *8 Songs for a mad king*
– Gyorgy Ligeti's *Aventures* and *Nouvelles aventures*

2 Instrumental sound bank

This activity is similar to Activity 1, but explores the sounds which can be obtained from various acoustic instruments. A bank of sounds is created, on which group pieces are based.

Preparation

This activity calls for acoustic instruments and, preferably, a tape recorder (see *D*): while the ancillary sections require commercial recordings (suggestions under *Further Study*).

Procedure

A Pass an acoustic instrument around the class, getting each student to produce from it a different sound.

B Discuss the sounds and make a list of them.

C Get pairs of students to choose two different acoustic instruments each.

D Get the pairs to find at least four different sounds from each of their two instruments, making a list of and/or recording the resulting sounds. [The recordings might be used again for var.i).

E Encourage each pair to experiment with its chosen sounds, trying different orderings, juxtapositions, intensities, etc.

F Get the pairs to produce compositions based on their chosen sounds.

G Perform the pieces in turn and discuss.

Variations and extensions

i) Get the pairs to make graphic scores of their compositions. Swap the scores around, getting each pair to recreate as closely as possible another's piece. Make use of the recordings made under *D*, so that every pair starts from the same basic material as the original composers.

ii) Further exploration of the unusual timbral possibilities of acoustic instruments is undertaken in Activities 9, 11 and 21.

Further study

The field of contemporary music offers many examples of extended instrumental techniques: perhaps the most concentrated study is the series of solo pieces by Luciano Berio with the title *Sequenza*; while Penderecki's *Threnody for the victims of Hiroshima* includes a wide variety of sounds available from stringed instruments.

    Parallels may be found in jazz (the use of the trumpet in its highest register); and in Indian music (the techniques used by tabla players to mimic the sound of the human voice).

3 One-note timbre

This activity involves pitched instruments and voices only. By using a single pitch in various registers, differences in tone colour are highlighted.

Preparation

This activity calls for:
- pitched instruments of various types
- a tape recorder

Procedure

A Each student chooses to sing or play an instrument. Where two instruments of the same kind are used, the players should be assigned different registers.

B A single pitch is chosen.

C Get a chosen student conductor to decide how this note is to be played/sung by everyone — short/long, loud/soft, accented.

D Record the players/singers, with the conductor bringing them in and out of the texture and directing them.

E   Repeat *C* and *D* until as many students as is practicable have had a turn at conducting.

F   Play back the recordings and compare the results.

Variations and extensions

i)   Let the conductor assign each individual player/singer a particular way of playing/singing the note — for instance: flute — *ff*/very short; clarinet — long trill and so on.

ii) Record the activity played/sung twice with exactly the same parameters, once by a group of similar instruments and once by a group of dissimilar ones. Compare the results.

iii) Pair voices with instruments — each vocalist to copy as closely as possible the sound made by the instrument.

Discussion points

–   Which hand signals were the most effective for this kind of conducting?
–   Which pieces were the most successful? Was this to do with the parameters chosen, the order of events, the combination of instruments, the self-confidence and skill of the conductor?

Further study

Good examples of music made up largely of single notes or small note-groups in widely contrasting tone colours are provided by pieces exploiting the so-called *Klangfarben-melodie* technique, essentially the Op.16 Orchestral Pieces by Schoenberg together with the sets emulating them by Webern (Opp.6 and 10) and Berg. Webern continued the technique into his serial period, useful examples being the Symphony (Op.21), Concerto for 9 instruments (Op.24) and (especially) the orchestral Variations (Op.30).

4 Open and closed

This activity explores the contrast between open sounds and dampened or closed sounds.

Preparation

This activity calls for:
–   pairs of the same instrument (some possibly prepared — see *B*)
–   materials (paper, cloth, rubber, plastic etc) for damping

Procedure

A   Distribute pairs of instruments (2 guitars, 2 drums etc.) to pairs of students.

B   Get the student pairs to explore different ways to dampen the sound of one of the instruments. On the guitar, for instance, the soundhole could be covered with cardboard, the strings muffled by the right hand, etc. (NB It may be advisable if some instruments are prepared in advance.)

C   Get each pair to play to the class a note with its chosen method of damping together with the same note on the undampened instrument.
D   Discuss each sound and modify as necessary.
E   In larger groups (3 pairs or more), get the students to explore the contrast of open and closed sounds and produce a piece exploiting them.
F   Perform and discuss the resulting pieces.

Variations and extensions

i)   Let the pieces produced in E exploit throughout the differences in closed sounds achieved by damping with different materials — hands, cloth, paper, plastic, rubber, etc. — as well as contrasting these closed sounds with open ones.

ii) As an alternative to group pieces, the whole class could produce a communal piece. A starting point for this might be to give each instrument pair a motif, shape or idea — for instance:

These could be used in various ways: one instrument of each pair playing the motif muted, the other open; selecting certain notes within the motif to be played muted.

iii) As ii), but experiment with different seating plans. Contrast an arrangement of pairs with two large groups, one of open instruments, the other of closed.

iv) Damping and other ways of sustaining and detaching sounds are explored in Unit 18, while materials such as paper, rubber etc. are used to "prepare" a piano in Unit 21.

v)   Discuss the technical distinction between damping (stopping the vibrations produced by an instrument) and muting (employing some means of changing the colour or dynamic level of a sound).

vi) Damping techniques are discussed in Unit 10 of two of the instrumental workbooks which complement this volume.

Discussion points

–   How does damping affect the timbre of an instrument?
–   In iii), how does the seating arrangement impact on the structure of the piece?

5 Monophonic style

The simplest texture is the single-line melody sung or played in unison, and this is the earliest textured music to have survived, often taking the form of solo sections contrasted with refrain section for all participants. In some traditional Chinese music, it is common to find a tune played in an octave unison style, with sections for tutti group and solo group alternating.

In this activity, students are encouraged to explore unison textures, basing their work on a traditional Chinese melody.

Preparation

This activity calls for:
- instruments
- tape recorder

while the ancillary sections require commercial recordings of birdsong pieces by Messiaen.

Procedure

A   The class should learn the following melody vocally, or an alteration (see var. v)

Traditional Chinese: *Song of the Oriole*

If they are learning from notation, it may be useful to do this in stages — first the rhythm, then pitches; if by ear, it may be necessary to shorten the piece, appropriate places to stop being bars 24 or 28.

B   Transfer the melody to instruments, being careful to use the different registers available; flutes, for instance, would be more effective in the higher octave.

C   Rehearse the piece as a full ensemble piece.

D   Explore the idea of sections for solo group alternating with sections for full ensemble.

E Add a simple rhythmic accompaniment, such as:

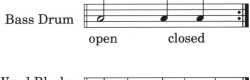

Bass Drum

open   closed

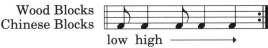

Wood Blocks
Chinese Blocks

low high ──────→

F When this is secure, record a performance.
G Replay and discuss, making any necessary or desirable modifications.

Variations and extensions

i) Add ornaments to the melody — acciaccaturas are both effective and in keeping with the style. For work on ornaments, see Activity 18 of Pitch and Melody.
ii) Compare this birdsong piece with birdsong-inspired works by Messiaen, in particular *Oiseaux exotiques* and *Catalogue d'oiseaux*.
iii) Activity 6 following itself forms a follow-up exercise.
iv) This alternation of solo and tutti sections in vocal tradition is discussed in Activity 22 of *Structure and Form*.
v) Alternative tunes to use: Chinese songs in Gaik See Chew: *The Dragon Boat* (Chester); traditional Irish music in *The Irish Fiddler* (Mozart Allen).

Discussion points

− In what ways does the piece live up to its title of *Song of the Oriole*?

6 Vocal monophony

This activity is a follow-up to Activity 5. One of the most important uses of music, from the earliest days, has been ritualistic, incantatory and liturgical. In this activity, students make up pieces for a predetermined function, using a monophonic style.

Preparation

Some preliminary listening to liturgical/ritualistic music (eg. Gregorian chant) may be desirable before this activity.

Procedure

A Get the students, in groups, to decide on a ritual function for which to provide music.
B Get the groups to select or invent texts appropriate to the chosen function.
C Get each group to choose a scale appropriate to the words. To begin with, it might be better to confine the choice to the pentatonic scale (major or minor).
D Have the groups set their words in a monophonic style, with sections for a lead vocalist (*Cantor*) and whole group (*Chorus*).
E Where in keeping, a sparse rhythmic accompaniment might be added.

Variations and extensions

i) There is much dramatic potential in this area. For some ideas along these lines, see *The dance and the drum* by E. & J. Paynter: the ideas in this book are designed for early secondary school use, but can be adapted for older students.

ii) For further ideas on spells and incantations, see Book I of G. Summerfield's *Voices* (Penguin).

Further study

There are many useful recordings of Gregorian chant, for instance *Tradition of Gregorian Chant* (DGG Archiv, 2723–071) and *A Guide to Gregorian Chant* (Vanguard, VSD 71217). This type of plainsong can be compared with ritualistic singing of other faiths, both Christian and non-Christian.

A more light-hearted example is provided by *Ego sum abbas*, No.13 in Orff's *Carmina burana*.

Activities 7–12

> **AIMS**
> 1 To explore the make-up of sound.
> 2 To explore vocal and instrumental timbres further.
> 3 To explore the effect of environment on sound.
> 4 To develop greater control over the intensity of sound.

7 Shaping dynamics

In this activity students develop their control over the dynamic intensities of acoustic instruments and/or voices.

Preparation

This activity calls for:
- acoustic instruments
- decibel meter (optional)
- prepared large flash cards showing dynamic contours against axes of volume and time in seconds, along the lines of:

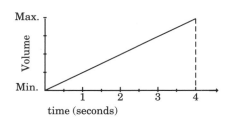
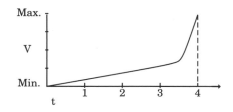

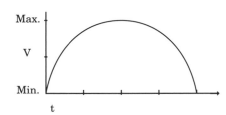
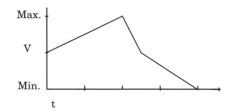

(NB. see also var.i)

Procedure

A   Working in a circle, get each student to explore the extreme dynamic parameters of an acoustic instrument or voice. Without loss of control, each student should play/sing the quietest and loudest possible sounds.

B   Repeat A several times to obtain a rank order for quiet sounds and loud sounds. A decibel meter could be used to measure the levels scientifically.

C   Display the results.

D   Select a common pitch and a set of hand signals to denote dynamic levels.

E   Get the class to play/sing the agreed pitch, with a chosen conductor shaping the ensemble's dynamic level.

F   Get the class, without a conductor, to follow dynamic contours on the prepared cards.

G   Repeat F with smaller groups.

Variations and extensions

i)   Replace the graphic notation of the flash cards with conventional symbols — **pp**, **f**, $<$ $>$ etc.

ii) In Activity 8 following, this shaping is used to give a sound envelope to taped sounds.

iii) Awareness and control of dynamics are further used in Activities 11 and 12.

Discussion points

– How far are dynamic intensity and pitch frequency related?

– How far is dynamic control an aspect of technical proficiency? Or is it a listening skill?

Further study

The short change of scene between scenes 2 & 3 of Act 3 of Berg's *Wozzeck* begins with the instruments entering one by one **pppp**, all (at pitch) on middle B, holding this note with a pause and getting as loud as they can. Then, after the bass drum has hammered out the rhythmic motif on which the whole of the next scene is based, the orchestra repeats the crescendo, but this time the B is at 3 different octaves, with much less intense effect (deliberately so). The second movement of Shostakovich's 15th Quartet begins with a sequence of 12 notes, each three seconds long and each marked **ppp** $<$ **sffff**.

8 Sound envelope

This activity forms a follow-up to Activity 7. In it taped sounds are shaped dynamically.

Preparation

This activity calls for:
- pairs of tape recorders (one of each pair must allow manual control of input recording levels) with connecting leads
- stopwatches (or watches with second hands)
- recordings of sound sources — these should be continuous and at a constant dynamic (continuous synthesiser presets would be suitable, try *flute* for instance)

while the ancillary sections require:
- instruments representative of the various ways of producing sound, or prerecorded sounds from such (var.i and ii)
- microphone(s) with long lead(s) (var.i)
- tape recorder capable of multi-speed (var.ii) and reverse (var.iii) operation
- synthesiser with envelope shaping capacity (eg. analogue machines such as the Roland Juno 60) (var.iv)

Procedure

A   Connect the tape recorder(s) loaded with continuous source sounds (Tape Machine I) to the recorder(s) with input controls (Tape Machine II).

B   With Tape Machine II in *record/pause* mode, begin playback on Tape Machine I.

C   Get the students (in groups according to machine availability) to experiment with shaping the dynamic of the source sounds by using the input level control on Tape Machine II and making use of the full range of levels (min. < max.) available.

D   Once this technique is mastered, repeat *C*, recording the results (by releasing the *record/pause* on Tape Machine II).

E   Replay the recorded examples, discussing the results in terms of:

a) attack rate — the length of time from the minimum sound level to its maximum point

b) sustain level — the length of time the sound is held at an apparently constant dynamic

c) decay rate — the time it takes for the sound to die away

The so-called *envelopes* of sound might be expressed in the form of graphs such as the following:

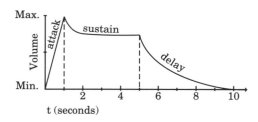 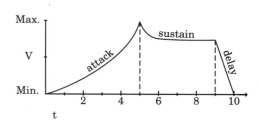

F   Get the students to design sound envelopes such as those above, and recreate them using the techniques learnt in *C* and *D*.

Variations and extensions

i) Use other source material. Try using "live" sounds and shaping them as you record. The sound of a cymbal, for instance, could be shaped either by using the tape machine's input controls, or by moving the microphone towards and away from the cymbal.

ii) Record short sounds from one blown, one bowed, one struck, one plucked instrument. Play the sounds back and see if a difference in the sound envelope can be heard. With a multi-speed tape machine, the sounds can be recorded at the highest speed setting and played back at the lowest: this results in a lower pitch (so record a high pitch to begin with), but allows more time to analyse the sound. Try to draw the envelope of each type of sound, marking the attack, sustain and decay components.

iii) Explore the effect of reversing the envelopes produced in *F* by recording the shapes backwards, or by reversing the direction of the tape on playback.

iv) Experiment with envelope shapers available on synthesisers.

Further study

For further advice and information on envelope shaping, see T. Dwyer's *Making Electronic Music* and R. Orton's *Electronic Music for Schools* (both Oxford University Press).

Nearly all electronic music has been shaped using this kind of technique, but the best examples are those using familiar sound sources, for instance Stockhausen's *Mikrophonie I*, where the sound of a live tam-tam is electronically manipulated. There is also the chord at the end of the Beatles album *Sgt. Pepper*, with its natural attack and electronically prolonged sustain and decay.

9 Contact points — wood, metal, skin

This activity explores the contrast between wood, metal and skin percussion instruments. It seeks to show the points of contact between these instruments.

Preparation

This activity calls for percussion instruments. There should be several contrasting examples, from each of the wood, metal and skin types.

Procedure

A   Form three percussion groups: one wood, one metal and one skin.

B   Get the students to choose instruments of the appropriate type, ensuring that there is sufficient contrast of sound within each group.

C   Using an ABC form, have each group in turn play a common riff pattern a given number of times. Here is an example of a riff pattern and possible instrumentation:

GROUP:	Wood	Metal	Skin
top line	claves	closed hi-hat	timbales roto-toms
middle line	wood block rubber beater	dampened cowbells	dampened floor tom
bottom line	gato drum xylophone	agogo bells chime bars	congas bongos

D   Expand *C* into a larger piece, incorporating sections where only similar sounding instruments from any of the groups play together. Contrast these with sections for the dissimilar instruments.

Variations and extensions

i) Adapt *C* using a different riff pattern for each timbral group.
ii) *Percussion Survey*
    Get the students to rank each instrument in each of the following continuums:

Duration:	longest ↔ shortest
Sound quality:	brightest ↔ dullest
Pitch:	highest ↔ lowest

Discussion points

– How can you change a percussion timbre? Is it possible to make a metal instrument sound like a wooden one?
– How far is the sound of a percussion instrument affected by the type of beater and the way it is used?

Further study

Albums by Max Roach's percussion group M'boom, for instance *Collage* (Soul Note SN 1059), are recommended for related listening.

10 Reverberations

In this activity students explore the effect of the different environments on sounds.

Preparation

This activity calls for several tape recorders.

Procedure

A   Divide the students into small groups according to the availability of tape recorders.

B   Explain that the groups are to produce and record exactly the same pattern of sounds in a given number of different locations, so that the differences in sound caused by the properties of the location can be analysed.

C   Get each group to work out and, if possible, precisely notate the pattern of sounds it will use. The pattern should contain plenty of short notes and gaps, for which reason easily portable wood percussion instruments (wood block, claves etc) are useful. It is imperative that the sound pattern generated at each location should be virtually identical.

D   Get each group to make a list of locations of contrasting types: closed/open spaces, high/low ceilings, bare/plushly-furnished rooms, stairwells, corridors etc.

E   Get each group to divide up responsibilities: for the recording; for generating the sound pattern; for keeping a log of the recordings, with the length and precise location of each.

F   When the groups have returned from the field, have each give an account of its findings.

G   Discuss the results.

Variations and extensions

i)   Repeat the exercise with the chosen sound pattern prerecorded. This guarantees the sound pattern generated at each location will be identical, but does mean that each group needs two tape recorders. Portable electronic instruments with inbuilt sequencers (eg. drum machine) could also be used, so long as the sounds chosen are not already treated with reverb.

ii) Experiment with electronic reverberation devices.

Discussion points

–   Is there an optimum playing environment for a given instrument/family of instruments?

Further study

Heavy reverberation is a feature of much reggae and Indian pop and is the basis of Lucier's *I am sitting in a room*. It is inescapable with any music performed or recorded in a large cathedral building.

11 Timbral survey

In this activity students make a survey of the instruments played by members of the class, or by other students within the school.

Procedure

A Get the students, working in pairs, to interview the instrumentalists in the class (or school as a whole) about the qualities of their instruments. A *pro forma* such as the following should be used for prompting the questions and recording the answers. The two examples of clarinet and tabla have been added as an illustration.

Instrument	Means of sound production	Materials	Pitch range/ transposing	Sustain/ dynamic	Timbral quality
Clarinet	Single reed blown	wood	F, > Bb''' transposing Bb, A, Eb	good sustain/ dynamic range	mellow, varies in pitch register
Tabla	Struck with hands, skin vibrations	skin RH drum- wood shell LH drum- copper shell	RH drum- often tuned to Sa (tonic) LH drum- lower-pitched, less precisely tuned	limited sustain/ dynamic range	Varies upon area of skin played and use of hands

B Get the class to collate the results and produce a master list.

12 Musical kaleidoscope

In this activity students play a board game in which they have to devise pieces of music spontaneously in response to symbols on the board. It aims to develop quick responses to musical stimuli.

Preparation

This activity calls for:
– a die
– a predesigned board, along the lines of:

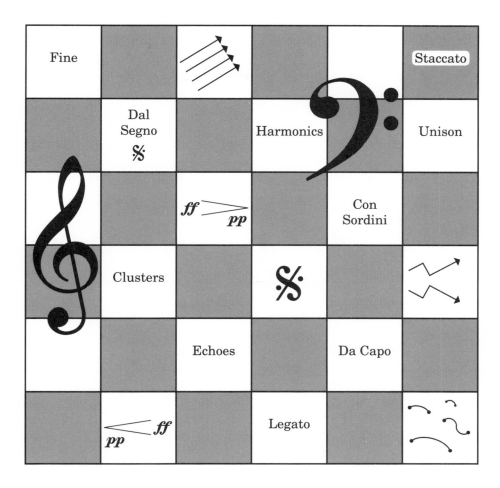

The board must include blank squares, squares containing musical symbols, a finishing square marked *FINE* and a starting point.

Procedure

A Devise rules for a musical boardgame to suit the symbols and configuration of your board's design: for instance, a board such as the example above, with its elongated treble and bass clefs, might be played like a game of *Snakes and Ladders*. Your rules should include the following elements:

- Each team is represented on the board by a token.
- Each team in turn throws the die and moves its token the corresponding number of squares.
- When a team lands on a square containing a symbol, they should perform a piece of music (of at least 10 seconds duration) which interprets that symbol. If the teacher feels the piece is successful the team may throw again.
- No piece is required when the token lands on a blank square.
- The winning team is the one that reaches the *FINE* sign first.

B Divide the students into teams of two or more and play the game according to these rules.

Variations and extensions

i) Many other kinds of symbol could be used: graphic notation; words expressing a mood (grief, love, anger etc.); Italian terms; well-known songs; names of composers/performers.

ii) Vary the instruments used, or use just voices, etc.

Activities 13—18

AIMS

1 To explore more complex textures.
2 To explore further the make-up of sound.
3 To develop further control over timbral parameters.

13 Counterpoint

In this activity students explore the layering of musical lines over an established slow-moving melody in the low register. It draws connections between music of the Balinese gamelan and the European Renaissance.

Preparation

This activity requires a tape recorder and (optionally) a multi-track tape recorder.

Procedure

A Get the students to invent a slow-moving melody. The melody should:
  – fit an 8-bar repeating frame
  – use only notes from a pre-determined scale
  – be constant in the rhythmic values used — crotchets or minims
  – keep to a lowish register (tenor range)
B The class sings the melody, either by ear or from notation.
C Get one group to repeat this melody, while one other student invents a second melody to go over the top of the first. The second melody should be quicker moving and more varied in its rhythms.
D The rest of the class learns the second melody, either by ear or from notation.
E Get two groups to sing the first and second melodies simultaneously, while a third student invents a third melody to fit with both.
F When the third melody has been learnt in its turn, get the class (in three groups) to perform the three melodies simultaneously.

G When this is secure, record a performance.
H Play the recording back, and discuss the result.
I Get the students to repeat the procedure in smaller groups, or individually using a multi-track tape recorder.

Variations and extensions

i) Analyse the two pieces following, in both of which the lower part serves as a nuclear melody around which one or more parts have been built. The first is part of an *organum* piece in the 12th-century Léonin style and should be sung:

Léonin style: *Benedicamus Domino*

The second is an arrangement of part of a piece for gamelan orchestra and should be played by metallophones or similar instruments (glockenspiels, chime bars, xylophones etc.). A simple unpitched percussion part could also be added.

ii) Compare the three-part texture of the Activity with the beginning of the slow movement of Beethoven's Symphony No.7 — see Activity 20.

iii) Repeat *A → H*, but at *E* only play the first melody. The second and third melodies are thus composed independently of each other, though each is still based on the first melody. This parallels a technique occasionally found in medieval music.

14 Sound clusters and open spaces

In this activity students explore the contrast between close-spaced textures and open ones.

Preparation

The Activity requires instruments.

Procedure

A Working in groups, get the students to select a set of neighbour notes (including semitones), for instance C, D♭, E♭, F, G♭.

B Get the groups to experiment with combinations of these notes in various registers, both closely spaced and open spaced.

C Using the results of their experiments, get the groups to compose pieces exploiting these textural contrasts. Any register(s) can be used: the pieces should explore the full range of densities from silence to saturation.

D Perform the pieces in turn.

E Discuss how each piece exploited and organised its contrasts.

Variations and extensions

i) At *C*, instead of performing its piece, each group writes a score. The scores are exchanged amongst the groups, rehearsed and performed.

ii) Experiment with different/similar timbral groupings. For instance, an all-string group could explore *glissando* movements from one note of the set to another. This could be especially effective if, in the case of the example given above, all began on E♭ and moved off in different directions and at different speeds, a quarter of the players to each of the other four notes.

Further study

Sound clusters feature in: Penderecki's *Threnody for the victims of Hiroshima*; in Bulgarian folk music, where it is common for vocal lines to contain many close-spaced dissonant textures (see, for instance, *Le mystère des voix Bulgares* vols.1 & 2); the piano textures of Charles Ives' song *Majority*; Act 3 Scene 4 of Berg's *Wozzeck*, which is entirely based on a single chord variously transposed and spaced. The harmonic style of some jazz pianists, for instance Thelonius Monk and Erroll Garner, at times comes perilously close to note clusters: listen, for example, to the opening of Garner's 1955 recordings of *I'll remember April* or *Mambo Carmel* or Thelonius Monk's *Monk's Dream*.

15 Sound montage

In this activity students make pieces based on recordings of natural or everyday sounds.

Preparation

This activity calls for:
- portable, battery-operated cassette tape recorders (at least 5)
- an external microphone
- (preferably) a multi-track tape recorder or mixing console

Procedure

A   Working in small groups, get the students to record (on separate cassette tapes) at least four everyday sounds — road noises, rustling leaves, unfolding crisp packets, boiling kettle, running water, machines, playground noises. The sounds captured should be of strongly contrasting types and each recording should last, if possible, for about four minutes.

B   Back in the classroom, play the resulting tapes simultaneously, using four tape recorders. Mix the sounds by using either the volume controls on the separate cassette machines or (if available) by linking them to a mixing console or four-track tape recorder.

C   Repeat B, experimenting to find the best mix.

D   When the best mix has been achieved, record on to a fifth tape recorder or the four-track tape recorder.

E   Play the recording back and discuss.

Variations and extensions

i) Record the original sounds on a reel-to-reel machine and make tape loops of each sounds (for detailed advice on tape loops, see T. Dwyer's *Making Electronic Music*). These could then be re-recorded on to a multi-track machine and mixed as in B ff. An alternative would be to use a battery-operated four-track recorder on which to gather the source material.

ii) Before the final recording is made (*D*), experiment with various auxiliary effects — filters to bring out certain frequencies, reverberation units to add depth. With a variable-speed tape machine the pitch of the sounds could be changed. The tape could also be reversed.

iii) With a sampler you could also capture sounds of short duration.
iv) Record and treat some commonplace sounds; then use the recordings to test the students' powers of perception and detection.
v) Relate this sound montage to montage techniques in other arts — painting, photography, cinema. This could be pursued as a joint project with other departments.
vi) Keep the tapes produced in this activity for possible re-use in Activity 23.

Further study

This kind of musical technique developed in the late 1940s, with the availability of practical recording machines using coated tape (as opposed to the steel wire used previously). The pioneers of this *musique concrète* were Pierre Henry and Pierre Schaeffer — listen to their *Symphonie pour un homme seul*. The technique continued to interest composers: John Cage, in *Williams Mix*, used sounds of the city, the country, the wind, etc, combined with electronically produced sounds. The Beatles, too, became interested in the idea, beginning with the fade-outs of numbers like *Good Morning* and *I am the walrus* and culminating in an entire track, *Revolution No.9* from the so-called *White Album*.

16 Sound spectrums

In this activity students investigate the relationships between sound and colour. Because of the subjective nature of perception in this area, it is designed as an individual rather than as a group activity.

Procedure

A   Get each student to produce two examples of light/bright sounds and two contrasting dull/dark sounds. Any instrument, instrumental combination or electronic sound(s) can be used.

B   Record the results and discuss how much the sounds in each category have anything in common.

C   Repeat A and B, every student producing four sounds, each of which should this time suggest to them a particular colour or shade.

Variations and extensions

i)   Play the students a variety of different sounds (notes, chords, extracts from pieces etc.) and get them to whether these evoke particular colours or shades of luminosity.

ii) Examine sound/colour associations in various areas:

instruments Do particular instruments or families of instruments have colour associations?

pitches Do individual pitches have colour associations? Both sound and light are founded on vibrations. In India some musicians associate pitches with colour, for instance *sa* = black, *pa* = yellow, *ni* = green, etc.

chords Can chords be described in colouristic terms? Messiaen frequently does so: he associates colours with his *modes of limited transposition* and with the chords derived from them. Listen, for instance, to his *Des canyons aux étoiles*.

keys Are certain keys brighter/duller than others? The Russian composers Rimsky-Korsakov and Skryabin both found they felt strong associations between key and colour, and defined the colour each key suggested to them. They had similar views on four keys:

Key	Rimsky-Korsakov	Skryabin
D major	yellow, sunny	yellow, brilliant
E major	blue, sapphire sparkling	bluish-white
A♭ major	greyish-violet	purple violet
E♭ major	dark, gloomy bluish-grey	steel colour, with a metallic lustre

Further study

The use of coloured light is of fundamental importance in the performance of Skryabin's *Prometheus* and Schoenberg's *Die glückliche Hand*, as it is, of course, in many popular music concerts (see the videos of the Houston and London concerts of Jean-Michel Jarre).

Colour imagery is prominent in many other pieces: Messiaen's *Des canyons aux étoiles*, Bliss' *A Colour Symphony*, Musorgsky's *Pictures from an exhibition* and Duke Ellington's *Mood Indigo*, *Black, Brown and Beige* and *Crescendo and Diminuendo in Blue*.

17 Harmonics

This activity explores harmonics, both natural and artificial.

Preparation

This activity calls for pitched instruments of various types — blown, bowed, plucked etc.

Procedure

A Divide the students into groups containing players of instruments from a range of instrumental families, for instance strings, woodwind, brass etc.

B Get the students to explore natural and artificial harmonics available on the instruments of their group.

C Get each group to form a sound bank of harmonics and create a piece exploiting these sounds — superimposing, reordering, contrasting them in different textures and at various dynamic levels. If this is found too constricting, the pieces could also incorporate normal sounds.

D Perform the resulting pieces in turn and discuss.

Variations and extensions

i) Try playing a simple tune in harmonics, using either a single instrument or one instrument for each note.

ii) Get a competent brass player to play or record some of the harmonic series obtainable from a low C. The notes should be, in order:

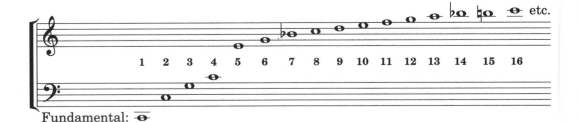

Fundamental: 𝅝

You could also compare these notes with the harmonics available from the C string of a viola or cello.

iii) See how far the students can obtain harmonics vocally. By singing a low note and varying the shape of the mouth it is possible to produce several notes from the harmonic series as overtones. (For instance, get the students to move the mouth very slowly from the position needed by the vowel a [*hay*] to that needed by o [*owe*], singing their low note throughout.)

iv) Harmonics can be demonstrated on the piano in two ways. *1.* Silently depress the triad formed by notes 4–6 of the harmonic series and then hit the fundamental note with a sharp staccato: the harmonics will continue after the fundamental has stopped. (Compare this sound with that produced by the same triad when note 2 of the harmonic series is struck.) *2.* Silently depress the octave C at the bottom of the series as shown above. Play all the white notes for three or more octaves above, either as a quick glissando or simultaneously using the forearm: a C major chord should emerge, the strings of the depressed notes vibrating in sympathy with each of the notes of its harmonic series sounded.

v) Experiment with the high harmonics that can be produced on a cymbal by playing the edge with a violin or cello bow.

Further study

Harmonics are covered in Unit 17 of the instrumental workbooks which complement this volume.

The vocal technique mentioned under iii) above is used in many contemporary works, notably Stockhausen's *Stimmung*. A tune played in stopped harmonics on the cello opens Shostakovich's Piano Trio No.2, while glissando harmonics are used prominently at the third tableau of Ravel's ballet *Daphnis et Chloé*. Britten's *Serenade* for tenor, horn and strings opens with a horn solo, which uses only the notes of the harmonic series and shows how note 7 as notated in the above series is only an approximation to the actual sound. The technique is used for humorous effect in *Personnages à longues oreilles* from Saint-Saëns' *Le carnaval des animaux*. For an example of harmonics on the bass guitar, listen to *Portrait of Tracy* from the album *Jaco Pastorius*.

18 Sustained and detached

This activity explores the sustain potential of instruments and contrasts this with short, detached sounds.

Preparation

This activity calls for instruments of a variety of types, preferably with widely different sustain potentials.

Procedure

A   Divide the students, each with an instrument, into groups of wide instrumental variety. Voices, too, can be used.

B   Working in circles, each student of each group makes the longest sound possible on their instrument.

C   The groups discuss and compare the results and the methods used — sustaining pedals (keyboards, vibraphone, electric guitar, etc), tremolos (struck instruments), circular breathing (wind instruments), air bag (bagpipes), bellows (organs, harmoniums, accordions, concertinas), amplification etc.

D   Repeat B and C with the shortest notes possible, again discussing the methods used — damping (see Activity 4), pizzicato (bowed instruments), removing resonators (marimba, vibraphone), etc.

E   Get the groups to experiment with these long and short notes, and produce pieces exploiting the similarities and contrasts between them.

F   Record, play back and discuss the resultant pieces.

Variations and extensions

i) Try building resonators for instruments with a short sustain, such as the wood block. Use a reverberant room to sustain the notes further and record the results.

ii) Consider the use of the sustaining pedal of the piano in such works as *La cathédrale engloutie* from Book 1 of Debussy's *Préludes*.

iii) Discuss the transformation of durations in Stockhausen's *Kontra-Punkte*.

Discussion points

– Can vibrato help to sustain notes on plucked instruments?

Activities 19—24

19 Folk song arrangements

In this activity students work on arrangements of two folk songs, Blow away the morning dew *and* The Cuckoo.

Preparation

This activity calls for:
– instruments
– tape recorder

Some preliminary work should have been done on the scales involved (see Activities 7 and 10 of *Pitch and Melody*) and on basic harmonisation (see Activities 5, 8, 12, 13, 19 and 20 of *Harmony*).

Procedure

A   Sing/play through the following folk songs:

Traditional English: *Blow away the morning dew*

There was a far-mer's son, kept sheep all on the hill, and
I   IV   I   V   I

he walked out one May morn-ing to see what he could kill. And sing
I   V   I   VI   II   V

blow a-way the morn-ing dew, the dew, and the dew.
I   IV   V   I   IV

Blow a-way the morn-ing dew, how sweet the winds do blow.
I   VI   II   Ic   V   I

Traditional English: *The Cuckoo*

O the cuc-koo she's a pret-ty bird, she— sing-eth as she flies. She—
I   III   ♭VII   I   IV   I

bring - eth   good— tid - ings, she— tell - eth   no— lies.   She—
I   III   ♭VII   I   IV   I

suck - eth   white — flow - ers for to   keep— her   voice— clear, and — the
III   ♭VII   IV   I   Vm

more   she— sing - eth   cuc - koo— the   sum - mer draw - eth   near.
I   III   IV   Vm   I

B   Get the students to identify the scales being used (G major and D natural minor).
C   Revise these scales and the chords derived from them.
D   Get the students (individually or in pairs) to add root chords under the melody. In
    most cases only one chord per bar is required, and nowhere more than two. Note
    that: i) the second piece is modal, so the chords used may not sound quite "right"
    compared with diatonic harmony, ii) some melody notes are passing notes, not
    meant to be harmonised.
E   Compare the student harmonisations and produce one definitive version. (The
    harmonisations given above are straightforward versions by the author.)
F   Get the students to write down the folk tunes on two staves. On the top stave
    (treble clef) they should write the melody, with all the stems going up. On the
    lower stave (bass clef) they should write the bass line, with all the stems going
    down. The bass line should consist of root notes, where possible moving in
    contrary motion to the melody.
G   Get the students to add two inner parts: alto, stems down, on the upper stave;
    tenor, stems up, on the lower. In each chord, the three notes of the triad should be
    present and one note (preferably the root, and not, where possible, the third of a
    major chord) doubled. The alto and tenor parts should supply whichever of these
    are missing from the melody and bass, trying always to move by step and avoid
    large leaps.
H   Sing through the arrangements in turn, the melody keeping the original words and
    the other parts using a vowel sound.
I   When these are secure, record, play back and discuss.

Variations and extensions

i) Instead of the students working out harmonies (*D* and *E*), play them the tune with chordal accompaniment such as the one given. Over several playings, get them to identify: where the chords change; which chords are major and which minor; the relation of each chord to the scale/key (ie. I, V etc.).

ii) Students more advanced in harmony could include inverted chords, or even produce an arrangement with the melody in one of the lower parts.

iii) Use different folk songs. A good source, with several modal examples, is *100 English Folk Songs*, edited by Cecil Sharp and reprinted by Dover Publications.

20 Instrumental arrangements

In this activity students experiment with different instrumental arrangements of a given three-part piece — the opening of the second movement of Beethoven's Symphony No.7.

Preparation

This activity calls for instruments, while the ancillary sections require commercial recordings of songs/pieces in contrasting versions (suggestions given under var.iii-v).

Procedure

A   Sing in turn through each line of the following, which are, respectively, the counter-melody, melody and bass from the opening of the Allegretto of Beethoven's Symphony No.7:

Allegretto ♩ = 76

* passing modulation to relative major

B   Repeat in three parts.
C   Get the students (individually or in pairs) to arrange the piece for a particular instrumental group. The instruments chosen must be ones played by members of the class. Care must be taken that the parts are within the range of the chosen instrument (see the results of Activity 11): if necessary the piece may be transposed. Students must also remember to write parts for transposing instruments in the appropriate key (again, see Activity 11).
D   Play through the arrangements in turn.
E   Get the students to develop these arrangements in some of the following ways:
    – double one or more parts at the octave
    – play through the piece three times, bringing in the parts one at a time
    – add a fourth, harmony part based on the chord sequence indicated
    – vary the rhythm of the bass part
    – swap over the top two parts so that the melody (middle part) is at the top

Variations and extensions

i)   Play a recording of the Beethoven original. Map out the way the material as printed above is developed there.
ii) An alternative (or additional) piece to arrange could be *Morning Mood* from Grieg's music to *Peer Gynt* (see Activity 4 of *Pitch and Melody* and Unit 12 of the various instrumental workbooks which complement this volume).
iii) Compare recordings of different versions of popular ballades. For instance, compare Stevie Wonder's own original version of *Never dreamed you'd leave in summer* (from the album *Looking Back*, Motown M804N3) with the version by Joan Baez (*The best of Joan Baez*, Hallmark SHM 3173).
iv) Compare recordings of different arrangements of a piece by the same composer. For instance: the three versions of Joe Jackson's *Is she really going out with him?* on the album *Joe Jackson Live* (A&M 6706); the two versions of the Beatles *Revolution* on the so-called *White Album* and as the B side of *Hey Jude*; and the arrangement of the Prelude from his E major Partita for unaccompanied violin which Bach made for organ and orchestra as the sinfonia to his Cantata No.29.
v)   Compare recordings of arrangements for different mediums: for instance Musorgsky's original piano work *Pictures from an exhibition* with arrangements of it for orchestra (by Ravel or Ashkenazy), brass band and organ; or Shostakovich's orchestral arrangement of *Tea for two* as *Tahiti Trot*.

Discussion points

– Which instruments work well together?
– How do the timbres of two different instruments change when they are combined?

21 Altered piano

In this activity students explore ways in which a piano can be altered or prepared so that its timbral spectrum is changed.

Preparation

This activity calls for:
- a piano with its lid and/or part of its casing removed to allow access to the strings
- a tray containing objects and materials which can be used to 'prepare' a piano — wood screws, rubber erasers, small pieces of wood, cardboard, paper, cloth, plastic, rubber bands, paper clips, foil, coins/tokens

NB. There is, of course, some danger of damage to the piano from this activity, if only to the tuning. It is clearly important that no hard objects are forced between the strings, and you may wish to choose the contents of the tray accordingly. Similarly, some LEAs are not keen on students using pianos as outlined below on health and safety grounds.

If you are unable, for any reason, to use a piano, it is possible to modify in similar ways the sound of other stringed instruments — guitars, zithers, violins etc.

Procedure

A   Get the students (working in threes and fours) to explore the effect on the sound of a piano note of placing various objects on the strings. Some objects may need to be cut to size.

B   Get each group to produce a piece based on its experimentation. The pieces could limit themselves to altered timbres, or contrast these with "normal" sounds.

C   Perform, record, play back and discuss the pieces.

Variations and extensions

i)   In addition to placing objects on the strings, students could play the strings with various (appropriate) beaters. A variety of wooden sounds are obtainable from the casing: for example, try hitting the casing with a *soft* beater with the sustaining pedal depressed. A piece could be made contrasting case sounds and string sounds. NB. Care should be taken not to damage the piano's delicate sounding board.

ii) Alter the piano sounds electronically, for instance by amplifying the sounds using a microphone which is moved about so that different intensities of sound are produced. These sounds could also be processed by filtering, delay, ring modulation etc., where available.

Further study

The name most associated with the "prepared piano" is that of John Cage. Contrast the sound of his *Sonatas and Interludes* (for prepared piano) and *Amores* (for prepared piano and percussion)(see LAM 109) with the timbres of a Balinese gamelan orchestra. In Stockhausen's *Mantra* the playing of two pianists is altered by live electronics, chiefly ring modulators. While in George Crumb's *Makrokosmos* (Volume Two) the piano is amplified and the player has also to use various unusual agents, such as paper and a wire brush.

The "honky-tonk" piano is a primitive example of (destructive) preparation, where tacks or drawing pins are pressed into the playing surface of the hammers. The sound has sometimes been used by classical composers, for instance Berg in Act 3 Scene 3 of *Wozzeck*.

22 New instruments

In this activity students design and make their own instruments. This is necessarily a large-scale project which is best undertaken in conjunction with the CDT department because of the considerable design and construction work it may entail. Alternatively, the activity could carry the project through only as far as the research and planning stage.

Procedure

A   Discuss with the class what constitutes a musical instrument, what an instrument needs to function as such. It should emerge from the discussion that, since sound is produced by the vibration of air, an instrument requires two necessary components for the production of that sound in usable form:
   – a controllable medium to set the air vibrating (for instance — a string, reed(s), vocal chords etc.)
   – a means of amplification (sound box, tube, casing, sound board etc.)
   It follows that the first of these will require an appropriate technique and/or agent to instigate/control the vibration (blowing, plucking; bow, beater). There are also several aspects of pitch: how is the instrument tuned; in what units are pitches available; how are different pitches achieved.
   It may be helpful to make a table listing these points and apply them to some familiar instruments. For instance:

Instrument:	*clarinet*	*violin*
vibrating medium	single reed	strings
method of activating the above	blowing	bow, plucking
amplifier	tube	sound box
tuning	length/thickness of barrel	pegs
pitches available	semitones	unlimited
pitch control	holes alter length of tube	fingers alter length of string

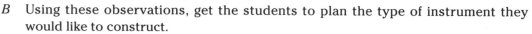

B   Using these observations, get the students to plan the type of instrument they would like to construct.
C   Get the students to make designs and discuss them with CDT staff, who should advise and oversee construction.

Variations and extensions

i)   Where construction is not being attempted, some study could be made of existing instruments which were designed to fit a particular niche (saxophone, Wagner tuba) or for their own sake (ondes martenot, theremin).

Further study

You can find advice on making instruments as follows:
– *acoustic instruments* in R. Roberts' *Musical instruments made to be played* (Dryad Press)

- *electronic instruments* in R. Orton's *Electronic Music for schools* (Oxford University Press)
- *thumb piano/talking drum* in the booklet attached to the Womad record *Africa* (Womad 003)

One of the most active creators of new instruments was the American composer and inventor Harry Partch. His instruments are discussed in his book *Genesis of a Music* (University of Wisconsin Press). Listen also to his *Study in the ancient Phrygian Scale*, which is played on an instrument of his own design.

23 Electro-acoustic exchanges

This activity seeks to draw connections between electronic and acoustic sounds, and explores transformations between the two mediums.

Preparation

This activity calls for:
- prepared tapes of various electronic sounds, including some *musique concrète* sounds: the sounds need to be simple enough to be imitated acoustically. The tapes from Activity 15 could be used here.
- a tape recorder
- means of creating electronic sounds and/or altering live sounds electronically

   while var.ii) requires modular synthesisers.

Procedure

A   Play a prepared tape to the whole class, getting some students to copy a sound (or several) either vocally or instrumentally. This may well involve some novel instrumental techniques.

B   Divide the class into groups, giving each a prepared tape.

C   Get each group to repeat *A* within the group.

D   Each group in turn plays to the class.

E   Discuss the results.

F   Get the students (still in groups) to design and create their own electronic sounds, producing a continuous tape which can be used with "live" acoustic music. (The sound montage material from Activity 15 might be re-used here.)

G   Get the groups to compose pieces which explore the continuum between electronic and acoustic sounds. It may be possible to achieve the effect where electronic sounds merge into acoustic and vice versa. Using live mixing/creation of electronic sound should also help here.

H   Perform the pieces in turn and discuss.

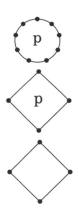

Variations and extensions

i)   Get the students to recreate some acoustic or natural sounds electronically, using modular synthesisers.

There are a number of works which combine live sounds and a prerecorded tape. One of the clearest for related listening is Stockhausen's *Kontakte*. Originally a piece for tape only, Stockhausen subsequently added parts for piano and percussionist.

24 Instrumental interchange

This activity explores the interaction of different textures, timbres, intensities and durations within an instrumental group and between several groups. It brings together many of the areas and techniques covered in this chapter.

Preparation

This activity calls for instruments (see *A*).

Procedure

A   Divide the students into two or three groups with (ideally) no more than five per group. Each group should have a similar make-up, with instruments/voices capable of producing between them a range of specified sounds, for instance:
 – open/closed sounds
 – sustained/detached sounds
 – word sounds
 – harmonics
 – 3-note clusters

B   Get each group to assign one of its players/singers to each of the specified sounds.

C   Get each player in turn to invent a 2-bar repeating riff (motif). It may be best to do this in stages, building up the riffs one on top of another by means of improvisation until the set is complete. The riffs must all be clearly audible and form a contrast with the others of the set: they should also each be simple enough to be picked up by ear. The following gives an idea of the sort of level required of the set of riffs.

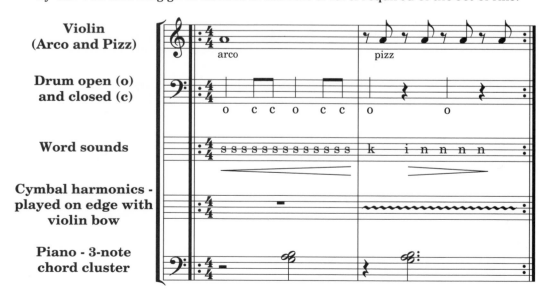

D   Repeat *C* to obtain a second set of riffs for each group.

E   Get the groups to rehearse the riff sets at least 16 times each. Each group might also experiment with the effect of varying the number of riffs being played at any one time.

F   Place the groups in the performance area available — a semicircular arrangement may be best.

G   Get Group A to perform its first riff set and Group B to respond to it: the open/closed sound specialist from Group B responds to the riff of the same specialist from Group A and so on. "Respond" here does not mean imitate exactly, but answer with similar ideas, timbres and textures.

H   Repeat *G* with Group A's second riff set: the Group B players should respond to the new ideas as quickly as possible.

I   Repeat *G* and *H*, with Group C responding to the riff sets of Group B, and so on. There should be a constant transfer of ideas between groups.

Variations and extensions

i)   Repeat *G–I* with the order of groups changed: B–C–A, C–A–B etc.

ii)   Use different sound parameters.

iii)   Get the groups to respond with dissimilar rather than similar ideas.

iv)   All the groups use the same riff sets, a conductor from each group determining the move from one set to the other.

v)   Construct a larger, antiphonal piece with a single conductor bringing in and taking out the various groups.

Further study

The following works, in which musical ideas are exchanged between groups, are recommended as related listening: amongst contemporary music, Berio's *Allelujah II*, Tavener's *Ultimos Ritos* (see LAM 119) and Stockhausen's *Gruppen*; and amongst renaissance antiphonal and polychoral music, Schütz' *Symphoniarum sacrarum, tertia pars* (see LAM 13) and motets by Giovanni Gabrieli such as *Plaudite* (for 12 voices in three choirs).

The layering of disparate groups of sounds is a feature of several works by Charles Ives, for instance *Three Places in New England* or *The Fourth of July* from his *Holidays Symphony*.

Index

This index cites only those activities where the topic in question is a/the major objective or concern.

The following abbreviations are used: RM *Rhythm and Metre*; PM *Pitch and Melody*; H *Harmony*; SF *Structure and Form*; TT *Timbre and Texture*; and EP *Ensemble Piece*. Thus RM4 means Activity 4 of the *Rhythm and Metre*, SF22 Activity 22 of *Structure and Form* and EP7 *Ensemble Piece No.7*.